PRAISE FOR
DARING TO CHANGE

"As a bilingual teacher, I applaud Helen Yoon for all the work she did to come to this country from Korea and to make such a difference in countless children's lives. Reading about the courage she found to change her career so she could find new ways to empower others will motivate people not to let anything hold them back from changing for the better themselves."

— Dana Arias, Author of
Dear Parents: From Your Child's Loving Teacher

"If you don't take action to make positive changes in your life, you're bound to have change hit you when you least expect it. Rather than be passive about your life, take charge by following the advice provided in Helen Yoon's inspiring new book *Daring to Change*. Her stories of overcoming obstacles and her instructive Dare Questions will help you make the changes you want and need to pursue your destiny on your own terms."

— Randy and Michelle Rosado, 9/11 Survivor, and
Authors of *Pursuing Your Destiny: How to Overcome Adversity and Achieve Your Dreams*

"Helen addresses some powerful themes for health and well-being in her book—change, personal empowerment, courage, and facing fear head-on. She speaks from personal experience as well as the experiences of others to help us all find our individual truths, passions, and creativity that lead to personal fulfillment. Health is more than absence of disease—this book will guide you in your quest for well-being!

— **Amanda Murphy, RN, HN-BC, www.wellnesspaths.com**

"While I teach readers how to clean up their homes, Helen Yoon teaches readers how to clean up their lives. *Daring to Change* helps people to focus on what they really want in life, to step beyond the clutter, and to pursue their dreams. Her story of how she changed, along with the many other inspiring stories of other adventurers and strong-willed people makes for great motivational reading."

— **Carol Paul, Author of *Team Clean***

"Helen Yoon is someone who knows what it is to dare to change and create your own destiny. She left her native Korea to study further to be an independent and respected woman, and eventually to live in California where she knew no one, and at a time when women in her native Korea were expected to be traditional wives and mothers. As a result, she became an educator and helped countless other students and parents transition to new lives of hope. *Daring to Change* can inspire you, no matter who you are, similarly o pursue your dream and live your life purpose."

— **Patrick Snow, International Best-Selling Author of *Creating Your Own Destiny* and *The Affluent Entrepreneur***

"Imagine being a young woman and leaving home, leaving your country, and coming all alone to a different country where you know no one and supporting yourself. That's exactly what Helen Yoon did when she came to the U.S. to further her education and pursue her dream. In *Daring to Change*, she will inspire you to do the same in pursuing your dream."

— **Seconde Nimenya, Author of *Evolving Through Adversity***

"When I read Helen's story in *Daring to Change* about how she pursued her dream by leaving Korea to come to the United States, I could not even imagine the courage that such a change took. And then she kept experiencing one change after another and continually saying 'Yes' to each challenge that presented itself to her as she became an educator and later a motivational speaker and leader of empowerment workshops. In addition, she is a lifelong learner who finds inspiration in others' stories of overcoming adversity. Many of those people's stories she shares in this book. She also offers practical and powerful ways to find your passion, overcome obstacles, and go on to become the person you've always dreamed of being. Best of all, Helen makes readers believe that if she could do all that, they can too."

— **Tyler R. Tichelaar, Ph.D.**
and Award-Winning Author of *The Best Place*

"If anyone knows about empowerment, it's Helen Yoon. Not only did she spend years empowering children in a multilingual environment as a teacher, but now she is dedicating herself to empowering adults through workshops and her wonderful new book *Daring to Change*. I'm confident many a life has been changed for the better through her efforts. Let your life be one of them!"

— **Karen Szillat, Educator and Author of**
Empowering the Children

"It takes courage and optimism about the future to make a daring change. In *Daring to Change*, Helen Yoon describes how she made a life-changing move in coming to the United States and all the success that followed for her once she dared to take that leap. Her story, the exercises in this book, and the steps she outlines for finding your passion and changing your life will make you want to pursue your dreams right away."

— Robin O'Grady, Author of *The Optimist's Edge*

"Helen Yoon has led a rich life, precisely because she has not let fear hold her back. In her book *Daring to Change*, she explores the steps it takes to change your life for the better. From finding your passion and turning it into your life's purpose, to moving mountains and seeing adversities as advantages, Helen will teach you how to change your life with courage and conviction so the changes are productive and lasting."

— Susan Friedmann, CSP, International Best-Selling Author of *Riches in Niches: How to Make it BIG in a small Market*

"Helen Yoon knows from profound personal experience what it is to overcome fear and make the changes necessary to create a new beginning. In *Daring to Change*, she will share with you how to live a life based on expressing your passions and life purpose. You will understand how to take the steps necessary to get there. Reading her story and taking her dare challenge to change will lift your heart to soar with hope and joy for a new day."

— Dr. Perry Chinn, Author of
Soaring Beyond Fear and *Symphony of Wellness*

"As Helen's supervising principal in the Los Angeles Unified School District, I found her to be an outstanding bilingual Korean/English speaking and writing teacher and a valuable staff member. Her abilities led her on to an administrative assignment in the district, in which she performed admirably. Over the many years I have known Helen professionally and personally, I have found her to be highly intelligent, knowledgeable, and of good character. Her personal experiences as an immigrant herself have given her a unique insight into the needs of other immigrants. Because she dared to change, her book, *Daring to Change*, is a valuable resource for anyone wishing to change, immigrant or not."

— **Raymond L. Howell, Retired Elementary School Principal**

DARING TO CHANGE

Empowering Yourself to Create the Life You Want

Helen Yoon

AVIVA
PUBLISHING
NEW YORK

Daring to Change
Empowering Yourself to Create the Life You Want
Copyright © 2014 Helen Yoon

All Rights Reserved. No part of this book may be used or reproduced in any manner whatsoever without the expressed written permission of the Author.

Address all inquiries to: creativehelen@msn.com

Published by:
Aviva Publishing
Lake Placid, NY
518-523-1320
www.avivapubs.com

Print ISBN: 978-1-938686-89-4
Library of Congress Control Number: 2013918011

Edited by: Tyler Tichelaar
Cover Design & Interior Layout: Fusion Creative Works, www.fusioncw.com

Printed in the United States of America.
First Edition

For additional copies, please visit:
www.DaringtoChange.com

Dedication

This book is dedicated to anyone who's ever wanted to dare to change, and to my mother, who devoted her life to her seven children, with love, patience, courage, gentleness, and compassion.

And to my father—we lost you, but your spirit is always with us.

Dedication

Acknowledgments

I am eternally grateful for meeting those wonderful people who kindly helped me and guided me as a self-supporting foreign student in this country so I could become who I am today: Young sun Yoon, Miss Lee, Minister Young Sook Lee, Dr. Young Ok Han, my guardian angel Doris Bond, Victor Hepburn, Mrs. Donald, Mrs. Hall, and Mary Gonzales.

Also I would like to thank my first principal, Mr. Ray Howell, who offered me the teaching position at the L.A. School District that changed my life direction, Mr. George DaVall, Principal, Hobart Blvd Elementary School, and Dr. Alan Crawford, Chair, Department of Elementary Education, California State University, Los Angeles for their support and guidance in my career.

I especially wish to thank author, Patrick Snow. Without his guidance and inspiration, this book may never have been written. And finally, I give special thanks to my masterful editor, Tyler Tichelaar, for his exceptional support, and my courageous mother who shared Korean War stories that held painful and fading memories.

Contents

Foreword by Tyler R. Tichelaar   15

Introduction   17

Part One: The Call and the Journey   **25**

    1: Igniting Your Desire and Dream   27

    2: Believing in Yourself   45

    3: Taking a Risk in Spite of Fears   59

Part Two: Finding Your Place in the World   **73**

    4: Finding the Spirit of Adventure   75

    5: Creating Your Vision with Intention   95

    6: Overcoming Obstacles and Adversities   109

Part Three: Miracles Do Happen   **125**

    7: Unfolding Your Destiny with Synchronicity   127

    8: Moving Mountains to Make It Happen   141

    9: Never Giving Up   157

Part Four: Transforming Your Life for the Next Chapter   **167**

    10: Living Your Passion and Finding Your Purpose   169

    11: Becoming Courageous   191

    12: Doing What You Love to Live the Life You Want   201

A Final Note: Will You Change?   **209**

About the Author   215

Foreword

Do you ever feel unhappy with the status quo? Do you feel stuck, or are you yearning for something?

Do you want to make a change, but you're fearful to do so? Do you ever feel like your dreams will never become reality?

Then you are reading the right book. *Daring to Change* will show you how you can change all of that. It will teach you how you can go from feeling like a victim to being the hero of your own life.

The author, Helen Yoon, knows how difficult and frightening change can be, but she also knows how wonderful it feels when you embrace your fear and make that change regardless, as she has done many times in her own life. She will share her own inspiring story and the compelling stories of many others with you to show you how to do the same.

The book *Daring to Change* will provide you with a clear roadmap to change. It will take you from your current destination of feeling unhappy and unfulfilled, and it will show you how to get to a place where you can live your life with passion and purpose, and feel that every day is a more wonderful, fun-filled adventure. Along the way, you will learn many ways to overcome your fear of change, step-by-step, including how to find your passion and turn it into your life purpose, how to move mountains when they get in your way, and how synchronicity works to help you achieve your dreams. Helen will show you everything you need to know to make your changes successful.

In these pages, you will find a compelling vision, courage, inspiration, passion, and purpose. As a result, you will see a new world open up for you. By the end of this book, I know you will have discovered that whatever change you are considering will be worth it for you. Then you will begin to take the steps necessary to live the life you want and deserve.

Once you begin to change, you will look back and realize you made the right decision. *Daring to Change* will confirm for you what you already know in your heart that you need to do, and I am certain it will make that change easier for you.

You are the only one who can make a change in your life. You can't expect it to happen otherwise. Be brave and let Helen guide you in embarking on your change with an adventurous spirit. I know you will enjoy the journey!

Tyler R. Tichelaar, Ph.D.
Award-Winning Author of *Narrow Lives* and *The Best Place*

Introduction

"You must be the change you wish to see in the world."
— Mahatma Gandhi

Are you unhappy with the status quo, feeling stuck, yearning for something, or fearful of making a change?

Change is going to enter your life no matter what you do. You can fear it or you can embrace it.

If you want to be in charge of your life, you have to be willing to dare to change before you are forced to or before you find yourself settling for unhappiness.

If you are currently unhappy, anxious, or feeling like you're searching for something that maybe seems impossible or difficult to find, then you are in need of a change. You probably already know that you need to make a change, but you might also be doubtful that it will make a difference, or you may feel too much anxiety about it to do so.

Daring to Change will guide you through the process of becoming the leader of your own life, so you will be in charge of your own destiny. In these pages, you will find the knowledge and the courage to improve the quality of your life and your work so you can make your innermost dreams come true. You will learn how to help yourself and others around you to grow and move forward by using your and their unlimited potential. You can make use of the power that you already have within you. You can make the decision now to change—a decision that can send you in a new and powerful direction for growth and happiness. You truly want to harness the power to create the vision and choose the beliefs that empower you, that allow you to step out of the old you and become a better and happier person so you can live the life you truly want.

Our ability to handle life's challenges is a measure of our strength of character. We do not learn those skills from school, but from our lives. As the oldest child of seven, I went through the Korean War, during which time I almost permanently lost my mother, and I grew up in a poverty-stricken country after the war. I learned then how life is precious and daily living can be hard. I know what it is to suffer and feel almost hopeless, but I found the courage to change so I no longer had to be a victim of life or someone who allowed change to catch me unprepared. The message of this book is that change is the essence of life. The purpose of this book

Introduction

is to help you change for the better, so you can have the best life possible.

In this book, you will discover inspiration, important wisdom, and tools for empowering yourself so you can enjoy the good things in life that you deserve, and so you can experience your life to the fullest. By the time you finish reading this book, it is my hope that you will have the courage to live bolder, to think bigger, and to make the changes needed so you can experience your life as being meaningful and fulfilling. *To change is a constant choice.* If you imagine the rest of your life being without a change, it will not be a life. It can only be stagnant.

It takes courage to face what is not working and bring about the change you need—to discover your life purpose, give conscious attention to your life and personal growth, and follow your heart.

Do you want to change? Then be clear and be bold about what you want. The key to change is to follow your compelling vision and your passion in spite of fear. Chase something so big and exciting that it's unimaginable to you and those around you. Be brave enough to take action, fail, get up again, and keep moving—this is living with courage, and it is the only approach to change that can help you to take off into a life truly lived.

Whether you want to start a new life, heal yourself from the past, or make a transition in your life, this book will help you to create the life you want. *Daring to Change* will guide you through the process of change. You'll find inspiring stories of others who have changed their lives and won the happiness and meaning they sought. And you'll get practical tips and guidance in the form of stories and questions that will help you through the difficult times. In these pages, I will share my own personal journey and many of my greatest pitfalls as well as triumphs with the purpose of helping you to change. I will also tell you many other people's compelling stories in the hopes that their examples of how they overcame adversities and made changes in their lives will inspire you to do whatever it is you now need to do to have the life you dream of having.

I know what it is to be where perhaps you are now—knowing you need to make a change but being afraid to do so. I understand your fear of change, your concerns, and your desire to move forward. I know what it takes to change as I have done it myself. I know because I made the huge change by moving to a foreign country. I left Korea when I was in my twenties. I came to the United States without any financial support from home and faced language barriers here while I worked on my Master's Degree. But making that change was worth it. I became an award-winning educator for over twenty-five years. Then I found a new meaning and purpose for my life, which brought another change when I became an empowerment seminar leader and motivational speaker who helps to transform other peoples' lives. Now I want to help you. I will be your coach along the way, your guide, your counter-partner. If I can do it, so can you.

Introduction

Are you ready to break through all your barriers and dare to live the life you want? Are you ready to begin with the first step? Let's plan out together the steps you need to take so you can pursue your dreams for your own life. This book will help you uncover new ideas, get out of your box, broaden your horizons, and help you pursue your dreams for your life. You will learn to overcome fears as you change your direction in life. In this book, we will explore the process of how you can change and what you need to know and understand to make successful change happen for you.

In Part One "The Call and the Journey," I will discuss how you can discover what your deepest desires are and how you can ignite them so your desires become dreams and your dreams become reality. Once we figure out what we desire, we have a roadmap for where we want to go, even if that journey may seem impossible. I will walk you through how to learn to believe in yourself, and I will inspire you with stories of others who believed in themselves to make their dreams become a reality. I will show you how even taking risks can be successful, and I will teach you how to overcome your fears so you can take those risks and begin your journey.

In Part Two, "Finding Your Place in the World," I will discuss how you do not need to focus on the fear, but now that you have taken the first step, you can move past it and begin your exciting new journey, filling yourself with the spirit of adventure and being open to all the possibilities available to you. As you see those possibilities, I will help you continue to focus on your vision and become more clear about what that vision is and how to achieve it.

Then we will break your vision down into steps to achieve it; I call this process "setting intentions." You will set your intention for each small goal along the way, so you have clear steps and actions to take to help you work toward achieving your ultimate vision. It will not always be easy; in the process, you will experience obstacles and adversities, but only if you choose to see them as such. Each problem that comes your way may be a challenge, but it's also an opportunity for you to learn, and it helps you become more clear about your vision and will help you further determine what intentions to set so you can move in a more focused manner toward your goal.

Next, in Part Three, "Miracles Do Happen," you will discover that when you are clear about your vision and set your intentions, and work on them with all your heart, the Universe is ready to return to you what it is that you seek. Suddenly, you will find that God is your co-creator. Unexpected coincidences may happen to help you achieve your dreams, but you will discover that those coincidences are really synchronicities and signs that God is working to help you. You will find that even when adversities come your way, good things will happen for you, and through faith and constancy, you will be able to move mountains that were standing in your way. Through perseverance and never giving up, you will find that the rewards you seek will come to you, just as if they were miracles. Finally, you will feel you have arrived where you want to be.

Introduction

In Part Four, "Transforming Your Life for the Next Chapter," you will discover that not only have you achieved your dream, but you have found your passion, and within that passion lies your life purpose. You will find courage to pursue your passion and make it your purpose. Best of all, you will be doing what you love to do and living the life you have always wanted, and you will be making the world a better place for everyone as a result.

This journey will not always be easy, but it will be exciting, fun, passionate, and purposeful. Along the way, you will be challenged and I will dare you to do things you might feel uncomfortable doing, but in the end, if you take the leap and dare to change, you will discover that your life is more amazing than you ever thought it could be.

Will you dare to change? It takes courage. Everyone has the power to make a change that will make a difference. Even if you're not sure what that change should be, if you have the courage, read on, and I believe you will find it. I dare you to change. I know you can do it. When you follow your courage, your life will blossom in amazing ways.

I send my deepest blessings that this book brings the inspiration you are seeking. I hope it changes your heart into believing that you can achieve anything you desire when you dare to change. Are you ready to begin? Let's go!

PART ONE

The Call and the Journey

CHAPTER 1

Igniting Your Desire and Dream

*"All our dreams can come true if we have
the courage to pursue them."*
— Walt Disney

What is the greatest thing you would dare to dream for your life?

What if you could ignite your desire or passion and make your dreams come true?

Every great success and accomplishment starts with a dream. In order to change anything in your life, you need to have a dream. Discover your deepest desires. Follow your dreams, and most of all, follow your heart.

Most people are not clear what their dreams are, or they don't believe their dreams will come true. They yearn for their dreams and think, "Maybe someday," but they do nothing to make those dreams become reality. You can start making your dreams come true now by becoming clear about what your dreams actually are.

First, find your deepest desires for what you most want to be, do, and have. You may not even know what you most deeply desire yet. If you don't, that's okay. I'll help you throughout this book.

Once you know what you desire, you need to figure out how to obtain it and what might stand in your way to stop you from getting it. One of the biggest obstacles we all face in obtaining our desires is our limiting beliefs. Limiting beliefs are feelings that you are not good enough to accomplish something or not deserving enough to have something you want. You must remove your limiting beliefs, which are stopping your dreams from coming true, and take action on your dreams.

Many of us define ourselves by our past circumstances, and those circumstances sometimes make us feel small and stop us from going after what we want in life. But no matter what your circumstances, there is a way to make a change, and this book will be your guide. You will find the inspiration and tools to create life as you want it. Remember, our past cannot determine our future when we declare the new thought and new dream. When you dwell on your dreams, your past cannot dictate your future. As the author Ralph Waldo Emerson said, "There is no planet, sun or star that could hold you if you but knew what you are."

Perhaps fear is what is holding you back from pursuing your dreams. The famous motivational speaker Tony Robbins said, "Life is found in the dance between your deepest desire and your greatest fear." You may have fears and obstacles right now that are getting in the way of you following your dreams or you may be thinking about following your dreams, but you keep postponing it because of current circumstances.

You might have self-limiting beliefs such as: "I don't have a college degree; I am too old to start living my dream, or it's safer for me to stay in my comfort zone." But you can look at pursuing your dreams this way: "What's the worst that could happen?" If you never try, you may always have regrets. If I hadn't had a compelling dream or the courage to leave South Korea, which was the only place I knew on earth, I wouldn't have had the experiences that I've written about in this book or be the personal growth leader I am, leading the empowerment seminars and workshops that I do now. Think about it. Weigh the pros and cons. Remember that old cliché, "Nothing ventured, nothing gained," and go apply it! A happy and successful life is made from making active choices and decisions. If not now, then when?

DARING TO CHANGE

Perhaps right now you are letting what other people think stop you from pursuing your dream. Perhaps others have told you that your dream is unreal or you are not good enough to succeed at it. Guess what? Those people are afraid to change and pursue their dreams, just like you might be. How do they know whether your dream is impossible if they haven't gone out and tried to pursue their dreams themselves?

Here's a case in point. In the book *Chicken Soup for the Soul*, Chuck Webster tells the story of Monty Roberts, a high school student who wanted to own his own ranch. When Monty wrote a detailed paper as a senior about his dream, the teacher gave him an F and told him it was an unrealistic dream. His teacher said if he would rewrite the paper with a more realistic goal, he would consider changing his grade. What did Monty do? He went home and thought about it; then he came back to school and told his teacher, "You can keep the F and I'll keep my dream." Later when Marty owned a ranch, his teacher came to visit. The teacher admitted that he was wrong and that Marty had been right not to give up on his dream.

Dare to dream the biggest and best dreams you can. You will do well and feel great when you act on your dream. Dare to pursue your dream and remember what author and philanthropist W. Clement Stone said, "Tell everyone what you want to do and someone will want to help you do it."

Igniting Your Desire and Dream

I have made major life decisions—marriage, divorce, a career change, and moving to another country by myself—all while in my twenties. The formative years—which is defined as being from birth to age twenty-eight, the years that decide who we will be as mature adults—were, for me, a time in my life when I had a strong internal drive for independence. I was compelled to pursue my dreams, fearlessly confident that anything was possible. Let me tell you the story of how I ignited and followed my dream.

I grew up as the oldest of seven children in a traditional household in Seoul, Korea. My father worked for several different companies as an accounting manager. Later, he became a small businessman who supplied construction materials for builders. My father was a hardworking and very disciplined man. He left for work early in the morning, no matter how late he had come home drunk the night before. I never saw him miss a day of work, including weekends. But he socialized with friends or business people after work so he would come home late, and drunk. He was handsome and a good singer. I am sure he was popular in his circle. But he was not always the husband or the father that his family needed.

My siblings and I didn't have a father in our lives to talk to and share experiences with because he was never around. Therefore, my mother was extremely unhappy. In addition, because my father was a dictator, she had no choice but to be submissive and tolerate with his behavior. As I was growing up, I became my mother's sounding board, listening to her sad stories; as a result, I feel I came to know the pain in life earlier than most. The good point about this may be that my neglectful father and his lack of a role in my life prepared me for the independent life I live now.

My mother was a full-time mother raising seven children. After the Korean War, South Korea was a very poor country, and my family struggled like everyone else. As the first of seven children, I was responsible for taking care of myself and my younger siblings when my mother had to go out. We went through the hardships of life during and after the Korean War since jobs were scarce and many people lost everything in the war. When we came back home to Seoul after the war, everything was stolen and destroyed, and even the wood floor was stripped. Jobs were hard to come by. Many people lost everything, and without work, they were on the streets begging for money or food. We had to sell our house in Kang Nam and move to a less expensive area that was also closer to my father's new job.

Through all these difficulties, my mother remained a warm, kind, funny, and compassionate woman. She had the most forgiving heart and was always patient with people. She knew every wife in the neighborhood, and she was a good listener, kind and humorous toward her neighbors, always making them laugh. In those days, poor women used to carry small items such as pure sesame oil, anchovies, dried fish, rice cakes, etc. in containers on their heads and sell them from door to door all day long without eating or drinking water. My mother would offer food to any of these vendors who came to the house during lunchtime. She would invite the lady to our table and they would eat lunch together. I was uncomfortable about eating with a stranger at the table, but Mother reminded me that these poor ladies would otherwise have no lunch. In this way, she taught me to be charitable and compassionate toward others.

My mother had grown up without a father from a very young age. He had been imprisoned from her childhood when she was in kindergarten while fighting for Korea's independence from Japan. The Japanese occupied the country from 1910 until the end of World War II. My grandfather owned a gold shop and he was supporting the fighters who were working for Korea's independence. One day, a Japanese soldier came and took him. That was the last time my mother saw her father. He was imprisoned until he died.

My mother was raised by her big brother, who was deeply compassionate and dedicated to her and their two other siblings. Like my uncle, my mother gave her total devotion to her family and she loved her children. Because she had always loved music, she made sure my sister and I learned to play the piano and violin when we were in middle school. We didn't have a piano at home, so I had to stay after school to practice. As a result of my mother's love for fine arts, I developed an appreciation for music and art early in my life. My music lessons and practicing also taught me self-discipline and concentration. My mom also helped me develop self-confidence through her constant interest in my life. She always listened to me when I told her about school, and she was eager to support my sister and me when we were in talent shows at church. After school, I couldn't wait to go home to talk to my mom about my school activities.

When I was about to start college, I had no idea what to major in, but my mom told me to study music since I had been taking piano lessons after middle school. Also music was her love yet she couldn't pursue it due to her family's circumstances. So I decided to major in piano in the music department. Then during my second year at college, I met a wonderful friend whose name was Kyung Ja. She was humble, thoughtful, had beautiful white skin, and great legs. Somehow she found me, and we became inseparable buddies.

Kyung Ja and I both majored in music under the same professor, and we were always spending time together. When we were on vacation from school, we used to see each other almost every day despite the rain or snow. Kyung Ja came from a well-to-do family, so her family could afford to buy her many things, but she was always moderate about her clothes, which made me comfortable around her. Nevertheless, I realized the difference in our families' wealth.

During my second year of college, my father's business was not doing well, and since there was no free education in Korea at that time, he had to take care of my younger siblings, who were attending middle and high school first. My mother told me to wait until there was money to pay my tuition, so I couldn't enroll in college again for the upcoming school year. I stayed home and waited without knowing what to do. Then one day, my dear friend, Kyung Ja, came to my house with the money for my tuition. I was so shocked to see her standing at my house, and I was embarrassed—I had never invited her to my home because we had such a humble house. At that time, we had no telephone at home, so she found out from the school that I hadn't paid the tuition yet and didn't show up at the class. She got my home address from school and traveled a long way to see me since she was living in Pil-dong, a wealthy neighborhood in the center of Seoul. She gave me the money for my tuition and I was so embarrassed to receive it. I will never forget her generous friendship, and I am so grateful to have had a friend like her.

To prevent being in a situation again where I couldn't pay my tuition, I decided to give piano lessons to help support myself, and I purchased a piano by making monthly payments.

It was a great feeling that I could contribute something toward helping myself by earning money.

During my college years in the 1960s, I was hearing about and seeing many pictures of U.S. President John F. Kennedy and his beautiful wife Jacqueline. I was so impressed by her beauty and her sophistication when it came to fine arts, literature, and fashion. She was a perfect socialite with beauty and grace, and she entertained the most talented and famous people. I began to yearn for a life like hers that seemed so far distant from the life I had. I felt I needed to go abroad to study if I wanted to learn to have that kind of sophistication. I dreamed about becoming a foreign ambassador's wife so I could travel all around the world and be a sophisticated, charming socialite. But that was only a dream, and at that time, I hadn't learned yet how to make my dreams come true.

Instead, after college, I married Jay, a childhood sweetheart, the son of my piano professor. I had started taking lessons from his mother when I was in junior high, so I met him at that time. He was waiting to see me at the gate with his friends every week on my lesson day. He frequently volunteered to be my bodyguard to keep away other boys who were following me and asking me to date them when I was walking to his home for my piano lessons. In those days, boys would ask girls, "Can you spare time for us to talk?" as a way of showing they wanted to date you. I had guys following me

Igniting Your Desire and Dream

from the bus, on the street, at the bakery shop, and at the pharmacy, etc. It was such a nuisance.

When Jay was a senior in high school, he came to see my father to let him know that he wanted to marry me when he grew up. My father chuckled and told him, "It is the time to study hard to prepare for your future; you are both too young to think about marriage yet." My father, however, was impressed by Jay's courage. When we went to college, we started going out during the second year, and we became good friends.

Jay's parents were both college professors, and they had three sons and no daughters. He was the oldest son, and a sweet, thoughtful man who was quiet and the deep thinker type; he was also rather a giving and listening person, who treated me like a princess in the relationship, which was very different from how my demanding father treated my mother.

Jay was generous with his time and lent his helping hands to my mother and my family whenever there were projects that needed to be done, such as fixing up an old fence. Since my father was absent in that regard, my mother appreciated Jay's help a great deal. My younger brothers and sisters also liked him as a brother. After our graduation and his completing his two-year ROTC military obligation, we got married.

Then on Christmas Eve, the second year after we were married, Jay left home in the early evening to meet his friends. He said he would come home soon so we could do something together. Because he was the first from his circle of friends to get married, they were always demanding that he join them. I accepted this and stayed home to wait for him, not knowing the exact time he would return or how to reach him since there were no cell phones in those days. He didn't come home until dawn the next morning. That Christmas Eve was the longest night of my life, filled with worries, anger, and disappointment instead of being a happy and exciting time to celebrate together with a family and loved ones.

When Jay came home, he tried to apologize and explain, but I didn't want to hear it. I knew he could not say "No" to his friends or whatever situations arose. And I suddenly woke up and realized that I was seeing my father's behavior all over again in my marriage. I was a young woman with a lot of anger toward my father and perhaps for men in general because of how my mother had been treated. My young husband had many good character traits, but I felt he was treating me like my father treated my mother after we got married. I suspected that most men behaved that way toward their wives, and I did not want to live like that.

I woke up in a state of shock, realizing my ideal picture of marriage was over. I deeply felt inside that I could not trust men and I didn't like the way they behaved. It was a heartbreaking experience. I had never imagined Jay could be that way when I had married him. After that day, something changed permanently in me.

I was stunned to find that I was in the same situation as my mother was in her marriage. I felt sad and angry for my mother, who couldn't change her life because of her children; if she got divorced, she had nowhere to go and there was nothing she would be able to do in Korea. I felt anger toward my father for being so domineering and disrespectful to her. I did not want to live the rest of my life like my mother had. So the next morning, I left to stay at my parents' house and take some time to think about my life. My parents were shocked to see me back home, and when I explained what had happened, my mother consoled me, and over and over, she told me to forget about the incident and stay in the marriage. Looking back, my father never said anything to me about the situation. He probably didn't know what to say to a young daughter who was leaving her husband. After all, he was behaving the same way toward his own wife.

I now felt challenged to make a powerful decision. I realized that I had as much education as most men did, unlike my mother who couldn't pursue her dream to go to college, and I was as capable as they were. I also knew I did not want to have a marriage like my mother had. I wanted to be an "independent and respected woman" and be free from the past and traditional Korean culture. I wanted to create my own life.

I then made the most daring and breakthrough decision of my life. With little money, no fluency in the English language, no traveling experience, and driven only by blind will, I chose to go to America, the land of opportunity, to live my dream of being an independent and respected woman.

I reshaped my life by getting a divorce and leaving for the United States while in my twenties. My destiny was to break with tradition and expand my personal horizons. To me, life should be one long nonconformist adventure. I pulled all my dreams and goals into one thought—freedom from the past to create my own life as I wanted it—my way. I decided to ignite my own passions and follow my own dreams no matter what!

Everyone in my family was shocked by my decision to get a divorce and leave the country for a new life. In those days, women did not leave their husbands. They would rather stay in the marriage than experience the shame of divorce. But I knew that ending my marriage was not ending my life—it was the start to a new beginning for me. I was free to go anywhere now, to create a new life as I wanted—to be an independent and respected woman. It was the biggest decision I had ever had to make at that young age.

Igniting Your Desire and Dream

The power of decision will immediately change your life. If you don't make decisions about how you are going to live your dream, you are making a decision to be directed by circumstances instead of shaping your own destiny. Instead, you can make use of the power that already resides in you. Make the decision now that can send you in a new, positive, and powerful direction for growth and happiness.

Dare Questions

When you were a child, what did you want to be when you grew up?

_____

As a grown-up, what do you still desire to be?

_____
_____
_____

How have your parents and childhood affected you as an adult? Did they get in the way of your dreams or encourage you to pursue them?

_____
_____
_____
_____
_____
_____

What experiences did you have as a child that influenced decisions you made in your life?

_____
_____
_____
_____

Igniting Your Desire and Dream

What dramatic changes have you made to live your dream? If you are not living your dream, what changes do you need to make so that dream can become your reality?

_____
_____
_____
_____
_____
_____

What are your passions? How might you pursue them?

_____
_____
_____
_____
_____
_____

CHAPTER 2

Believing in Yourself

"You have to believe in yourself when no one else does. That's what makes you a winner."
— Venus Williams, Olympic gold medalist

Anything is possible, but first *you must believe in it.*

Most of us define ourselves by our past. We think who we are is the sum of what happened to us in the past, such as: I am a divorcee, I was not the best student, I had no money. We let those events limit us.

If you want to change, the first thing you need to do is remove what stands in your way, and that means letting go of your limiting beliefs. Tony Robbins, the famous motivational speaker, says about limiting beliefs, "Our beliefs are like unquestioned commands, telling us how things are, what's possible and what's impossible, what we can and cannot do. They shape every action, every thought, and every feeling that we experience." As a result, changing our belief system is central to making any real and lasting change in our lives. Author and inspirational speaker Wayne Dyer said, "The only limits you have are the limits you believe."

We can choose to use the power within us to say "No" to past and present disempowering thoughts, and then allow a new life dream to manifest in our lives with empowering beliefs and a sense of certainty. As Dr. Benjamin Spock said, "Trust yourself. You know more than you think you do." It takes trust to be comfortable with yourself. In doing so, you acknowledge and accept yourself despite what others think. Take pride in who you are and others will treat you the same way. Remember, nothing changes unless you get up and start doing new things to bring about change.

I knew my life couldn't change unless I made it happen, so I decided to leave Korea and pursue my dream of a different life than what my mother had known; she had no say in her traditional marriage and she could not get a job and change her situation when she had seven children. I was just not willing to live like she did. I wanted to create a new life that could be anything I wanted as an independent woman.

Believing in Yourself

I couldn't count on my family much to help me once I started college or after that time, so I began making decisions for myself. I took jobs as a piano teacher or a live-in teacher who tutored students. The one lasting benefit of being forced to stand on your own at an early age—because, of course, there's a bright side to everything—is that you are that much better able to handle yourself later on in life. Because I had to support myself and make my own decisions, it made me stronger and gave me the courage eventually to go to America.

Your strong will is not compatible with wimpy behavior, so don't be afraid to follow your own course of action. Once you have mastered the lesson of independence, you will be armed with the courage to face whatever comes your way without having to rely on anyone else.

Believing in yourself is an exciting adventure, an opportunity to explore your own gifts. What you believe you can create. When you want to succeed in anything, you have to have a strong passion and develop a strong conviction that you have what it takes. You have to believe that you are capable of making it happen.

You need to believe that you can do anything you put your mind to. You can make use of the power of persistence, discipline, and determination that reside within you. Make the decision now with a strong faith that you will achieve whatever goal you have. Then your faith will send you in a new and powerful direction. You need to find your own passion, goals, and desires, not the ones you took from your parents, spouse, or friends. Have the courage to face whatever comes your way without having to rely on anyone else. You may co-create with God or the universe as I did. By co-creating, I mean trusting in God or the universe to help you find your path even if you don't know yourself what it might be.

The universe can assist you only when you are clear and passionate about your dream. When you set out on your dream, the how's—the answers to how to make it happen—will show up as you move into the next step. While I didn't know how I would accomplish my dream yet, I was clear about my dream to become an "independent and respected woman."

One morning after my divorce and while I was staying with my parents, I looked in the mirror and said to myself, "Your life is up to you." I was ready to own my life and accept myself and be the person I wanted to be. I didn't yet know how this would happen, however. Then one day, my best friend, Kyung Ja, told me that an interior design office was going to be opening in Myung Dong, in the center of Seoul, which had the fanciest shops, similar to Rodeo Drive in Beverly Hills, Los Angeles.

I was so excited to hear about this opportunity. I appreciated beauty, and in college, I'd become devoted to making spaces beautiful. I used to rearrange the furniture and change the wallpaper in my room so often that my mother jokingly repeated the old maid's tale, "People like you would change their spouses." Little did she know then how right she was.

At that time, we were living in a newly built house with a big yard, so I developed a love for gardening. Every spring, I would till the soil, plant a variety of seeds for different kinds of flowers, and after they sprouted, I would rearrange them according to colors and sizes. On the window, I would place thread for the morning glories to climb so we could appreciate them when they would open and smile at us in the morning. After I left home, my mother really missed my gardening because no one else was interested in doing it, so she didn't get to enjoy the many blooming flowers anymore.

Now, I began to think about studying interior design and working in what was a new field at that time. I decided, however, that I needed to go to the U.S. to study so I could be an independent woman who could create her own life, something not readily possible in Korea in those days.

America was an ideal country for me because it was the land of opportunity, freedom, and equal treatment for women and men, divorced or not, and a rich country with generous and kind people, as I knew from the missionaries from

America who had visited Korea. Plus, English was the foreign language I knew best.

Around that time, my younger sister's fiancé and my future brother-in-law, Captain Han, went to the U.S. to work on his master and doctoral degrees. He had a scholarship from the Korean government. Since he was already in the U.S., he inspired me to believe I could go there as well. Until that time, I had never traveled anywhere beyond Seoul. Therefore, I felt more secure about going to America because I would know someone there.

My brother-in-law was a model for me of how to overcome adversity. He was the first son of nine children from a modest family in the province. He was diligent, bright, and had believed that he could achieve his goal to enter the military academy and serve his country. When he graduated from the military academy as the second honorary student, he received a scholarship for earning his master's and doctorate in the United States. My sister and he were engaged for five years while he was away—what a commitment and love they had for each other! He was also a family man, unlike my father, so my sister was very lucky to have met him. When my brother-in-law returned to Korea, he became a chemistry professor at the military academy, and later he was promoted to being General Han in Korea.

Believing in Yourself

I had great respect for my future brother-in-law. He had a strong commitment and was persistent in his quest to achieve his goals. His success came from believing he could do anything to which he put his mind. When I contacted him and told him I wanted to go to the United States, he helped me get through the student visa procedure that would allow me to study in the U.S. He was my hero, and I am eternally grateful for his advice and help.

Of course, I asked for my parents to give me permission to go to the U.S. to study. It was very hard for them to send a young daughter to a foreign country where the language and culture were very different, and there were no funds to support me, but they honored my compelling desire, and I will be forever grateful for their consent and their support of my dream. I thought my father was like many other fathers in those days, a stuffy traditional Korean man who wouldn't allow a young daughter to go to school alone in a foreign country. But today I realize my father was pretty open-minded about my decision.

When I gave my friend, Kyung Ja, the bombshell news that I was going to America, she was so shocked. She wanted to follow me to study in the United States, but her parents wanted her to marry. They didn't want their daughter to become an old maid. After I left, I missed her, my buddy, and the friendship that we had shared.

I had approximately $2,000 that I had saved from giving piano lessons to take with me. I left home with one bag of clothes. I felt so sorry for my mother, who was losing not only her first daughter who was like a strong son, but her listener, and a friend to talk to from her deepest heart. But I also realized I could not remain and live my life solely for her or anyone else, and at the same time, I didn't want to be a burden and constant pain for my parents. As the plane was taking off from Kim Po airport, I wanted to embrace the future with a belief that anything was possible, and I was ready for it with all my heart. I prayed that everything would be fine.

Remember, when you set out on pursuing your dream, the how's will show up as you move into the next step. I was on my way to achieving my dreams now because I had believed in myself, and my brother-in-law had helped to pave the way for me. If you ask successful people how they got to where they are, every one of them is bound to tell you about the importance of believing in yourself. Following are a few more stories as examples of how believing in yourself can help you to succeed.

BE HUNGRY FOR YOUR DREAM: LES BROWN

Today, Les Brown is one of the most successful motivational speakers in the United States. But he didn't start out successful. Les and his twin brother, Wesley, were born on a

Believing in Yourself

cold cement floor in the building and then left there by their mother. Then they were adopted when they were six weeks old by a single, thirty-eight-year-old woman. She worked in a cafeteria as a cook and domestic worker, and she had very little education or financial means, but she had a very big heart and the desire to care for Les and Wesley. Les failed at school; he was labeled as being educable mentally retarded and downgraded to fourth grade from fifth grade. In high school, he was in special education and had no hope of a college education. Due to his inattention to his schoolwork and his restless energy, he was referred to as "D.T." for "dumb town."

But Les had a dream and he believed it was possible. His dream was buying a house for his mother and providing for her so she wouldn't have to go to work every day. As Abraham Lincoln said, "All I have and will hope to be, I owe to my mother." Les Brown felt the same way about his mother.

Another dream Les Brown had was to become a disc jockey. He loved broadcast radio. Every day he went to the nearby radio station to ask for a job in broadcasting. Meanwhile, he was listening to the program, developing vocabulary, observing the disc jockey in the control room, and practicing daily for the opportunity.

Finally, after his consistent effort daily in asking for a job, the manager gave him a job of delivering food to the office and control room where he could watch and memorize things the disc jockey did. Les became a driver for the celebrities who were visiting the station. Then one day, the disc jockey was drinking on the job and couldn't finish the program. So the manager called Les and told him to find another disc jockey, but Les thought this was his moment. He called his mom to listen to the radio and he called the manager and told him no one was available. Then the radio station's manager said, "You can do it since you have been familiar with it by watching daily." And the rest was history as Les launched his career in broadcasting, and became an author, motivational speaker, and a politician, including being a member of the Ohio House of Representatives.

As Les says, "Be bold" and "Be hungry" for your dream. He also says, "Eighty-seven percent of people fail because they don't believe in themselves. And all things are possible if you only believe. You are the star and you write your own life. Don't worry about your age, and say yes to your dream."

Every great invention was once an impossible dream. Every great event or success that has ever happened was also once a seemingly impossible dream. Here are some more examples:

- Martin Luther King Jr. believed there could be peace between the races in America.

- John F. Kennedy believed the United States could land a man on the moon within ten years.

- The Founding Fathers of the United States believed they could create a new nation based on freedom, even though it meant rebelling against Great Britain, which was the world power at the time.

- Germans believed the Berlin Wall could be brought down.

Impossible beliefs can become possible when you take action to create what you want. There is plenty of action involved. Start with a belief, a vision, an intention, and then take an action.

Believing in Your Vision: Dr. Thomas Han

When he was twelve years old, Thomas Han came to America from Korea with his mother. After just a year, his mother passed away, and Thomas found himself an orphan at a young age in a new and unfamiliar country. At that time, Thomas and his mother had been renting an apartment from Mr. George Okee Owend, a second generation Japanese man. Mr. Okee had several apartments to look after and his children were all grown up and had moved out, so he decided to become Thomas' guardian and have Thomas help him. He taught Thomas gardening and painting, paid him for his work, and only charged him $50 rent to stay in the apartment he'd shared with his mother. As a result, Thomas learned responsibility.

To earn extra money, Thomas also found a job distributing newspapers. One day, a newspaper subscriber, who didn't want to pay his bill, beat up Thomas. The boy came home with bruises all over his body. Mr. Okee, seeing what had happened, took Thomas to the Chinese karate studio for lessons every week after that.

When Thomas finished high school, he joined the air force. In the meantime, he studied for college credits and gained a medical technician certificate. When he finished his four-year-term in the military, he enrolled at the University of California-Irvine and studied biology. His mother had once held the dream for him that he would become a famous scientist, so he was determined not to let her down. He went on to earn a Master's degree at UCLA, studying periodontal science, and while he was going to school, he also had a night job working in the lab twenty hours a week. Ultimately, he received many awards from professional organizations, and besides being a periodontal surgeon, he was a professor at UCLA.

Although he began his life as a young orphan in a foreign country, Dr. Thomas Han has been quoted as saying that he does not think he had a hard life, but rather that he has been a fortunate person. He attributes his success in life to the fact that he had the vision to live his mother's wish to be a famous scientist. Later, he became a well-respected periodontist and professor in his field because he never stopped believing in himself.

Dare Questions

What opportunities are you faced with currently?

_____
_____
_____

What limiting beliefs do you have that are keeping you from pursuing those opportunities?

_____
_____
_____
_____

What positive beliefs do you hold about yourself that you can use to empower your life?

_____
_____
_____
_____

What are three seemingly impossible things that you believe you can make happen within the next month by taking action?

_____
_____
_____
_____

CHAPTER 3

Taking a Risk in Spite of Fears

"The quality of our lives improves in direct proportion to our ability to take on challenging risks."
— Bill Treasurer

We often find ourselves caught in the tension between wanting change and fearing change. Life equals risk. It is a simple fact. However, no one ever achieved greatness without taking a risk. Taking a risk can be scary—there is the possibility of failing miserably. However, our success and great pleasure of accomplishment come when we challenge our beliefs, convictions, and comfort zones. When fear stops us from taking a risk, it holds us back from being our best. Being fearless is not the absence of fear; being fearless means having the courage to move forward, to think new thoughts, try new things, start over, and take risks, no matter what.

Arianna Huffington knows what it is to take risks. She was raised in Greece by her fearless mother. Her dream was to attend Cambridge University and the university's famed debating society. But she had to overcome the barrier of having a heavy Greek accent in a world where accents really mattered. More importantly, she had to overcome the fear of criticism and ridicule due to her heavy accent. If she didn't, she knew she would never be able to speak fearlessly in public.

Ultimately, Arianna became a fearless woman who wrote eleven books, ran for governor in California against Arnold Schwarzenegger who won the election, and launched the *Huffington Post*, which became a successful online source of news and opinion. In 2006, she was named by *TIME* magazine as one of the most influential people in the world.

In her book, *On Becoming Fearless,* she said:

> Fearlessness is about getting up one more time than we fall down. The more comfortable we are with the possibility of falling down, the less worried we are of what people will think if and when we do, the less judgmental of ourselves we are every time we make a mistake, the more fearless we will be, and the easier our journey will become.

Taking a Risk in Spite of Fears

Just as all successful people have had to believe in themselves, they've had to take risks to achieve success. Several other famous people have confirmed the importance of risk-taking. Herbert A. Otto, author and psychiatrist, states, "Change and growth take place when a person has risked himself and dares to become involved with experimenting with his own life." Motivational speaker Les Brown has said, "You don't grow if you are not willing to risk." Here are just a few examples of famous people who have taken risks and succeeded:

- Thomas Edison had a teacher who said he was too stupid to learn anything. Edison went on to invent the lightbulb and numerous other inventions that revolutionized the world. Yet people believed the lightbulb could not succeed and Edison repeatedly failed before he succeeded. He is known to have said, "I have not failed. I've just found 10,000 ways that won't work." What if Edison had feared change? We would still be reading by candlelight after sundown.

- Walt Disney was fired from a newspaper job because he was said to have a lack of imagination and had no original ideas. But he had a great vision to create animated films, and later, a great amusement park, Disneyland.

- Abraham Lincoln, the sixteenth president of the United States, had a fiancée who died, had two failed businesses, had a nervous breakdown, and was defeated in elections several times. His response to failure and risk-taking: "If you never failed, you never lived." If he had been afraid of change, he would not have signed the Emancipation Proclamation and slavery would have continued in the United States.

When you take risks, it helps to enrich your character, strengthen your courage, and further develop your risk-taking abilities. Of course, not everyone is a Thomas Edison or a Walt Disney, but we all have dreams, and we understand those dreams can't come true if we don't take risks. And every time we take a risk, we become a greater believer in ourselves and the potential for success. Let me give you a personal example:

I was participating in Tony Robbins' seminar called, "Unleash the Power Within" at the Pasadena Civic Center in the 1980s. Almost a thousand people were packed into the auditorium. After three days of the seminar, we had to walk on burning coals to master our fears. We had to take off our socks to walk on the fire because, otherwise, the socks could catch on fire. Looking at the red, burning coals, I was freaking out and decided just to go home. But I saw there were many people lining up to walk on the fire. I felt like I would be a failure if I did not walk on the fire. So I got in the line and followed the instruction: "Don't look down, but look at the instructor's finger at the end of the line." The first time I walked on the red burning coals without burning my feet, I was so shocked. I wanted to do it again to feel it was real. I focused on the power of finishing the walk instead of my fear of burning, and I passed the second time. It was an amazing experience

Taking a Risk in Spite of Fears

that made me feel I could do anything if I put my full heart into it with a spirit of adventure and belief that anything is possible.

As you step beyond your comfort zone into unfamiliar ground, new possibilities will show up for you to feel and experience how powerful, resourceful, brave, and amazing you really are. Courage and a risk-taking spirit open up new possibilities. Take a risk despite the fear. The more risks you take, the more courageous life you can create.

When I was in my twenties, I took the biggest risk of my life so far when I decided to come to the United States to begin a new life. Once I arrived in the United States, I would have no financial support from home, and I would have no one to help me adjust to life in a foreign country. I was at a crucial moment. I needed to be courageous. I couldn't depend on anyone else to do anything for me. Change was frightening, but I knew I had to be the initiator of my own destiny.

I had never flown or left my family before until the moment I boarded the plane for the U.S. with little more than my dream and the prospect of an unknown country before me. Somehow, I would create a new beginning for myself—in a land with a totally different language and culture. I was taking a big risk—one beyond my imagination. But I was thinking to myself, "It can't be worse than living as a divorced young woman in the traditional culture of my own country!"

DARING TO CHANGE

I knew in my heart that I would try whatever it took to create a new beginning anywhere, as long as I had the chance to live my dream and to be an independent and respected woman. I was going to the U.S. with a compelling vision—to study interior design and become the first Korean woman to study in the U.S. in that field.

My flight would take me to Denver, Colorado, where I would stay with my future brother-in-law for three weeks before going to Los Angeles, where I would be attending school. When I finally arrived in Denver, it was late fall and cold. My future brother-in-law came to pick me up from the airport. For the first twenty days, I stayed in the university town of Boulder, Colorado with him and the American family he stayed with. He showed me around Boulder, which I thought was such a peaceful and beautiful city with colorful foliage and gorgeous mountains. He took me to the university campus and introduced me to his American professors. It was very strange for me to meet them because they all looked alike to me. I couldn't remember who was who. That was the first of many culture shocks I would have in the U.S.

My brother-in-law had been the one who wisely suggested I study in Los Angeles because there were more Koreans living there. He thought I would find more help and support among other Koreans. At that time, only five Korean students were at the University of Colorado and they were on scholarships from the government. Many of them would leave soon.

Taking a Risk in Spite of Fears

After twenty good days in Colorado, I needed to leave for Los Angeles to go to school, but I did not know a soul in L.A. I had one friend living in Chicago at that time, so I called her up. I felt so excited and lucky when she answered and told me she had a friend in South Pasadena, which was not far from L.A. She arranged for her friend to pick me up at the airport. I was so excited and felt so lucky that I would have at least one person to talk to.

When I arrived at the Los Angeles airport, however, I was totally lost. I had never seen an airport that big. Everything was new to me, especially the escalator. We didn't have any escalators in Korea at that time. I finally found the baggage stand and got my bag. I was looking around for Miss Lee, whom I had never met, but there were no Asians in sight.

I anxiously waited for over an hour, holding tightly onto my one bag, but no Miss Lee was in sight. Finally, I decided to take the escalator to the second floor. Halfway up, I saw an Asian lady who was coming down the escalator and looking in another direction. Since we were far apart and moving in opposite directions, I yelled out in desperation, "Are you Miss Lee?" She said, "Yes," and asked, "Are you Miss Yoon?" "Yes, I am!" I replied. My new life started at that incredible juncture. Miss Lee was a cute and short lady who was full of energy and laughter. I was so happy to meet her and felt so thankful to have someone like her to help me. I felt like she was my guide, like the older sister I had never had.

Many years later, whenever I told my teacher colleagues my story at lunchtime about being at the Los Angeles International Airport, not knowing a soul in L.A., they told me I should write a book. I laughed and thought they were joking. Now I am finally writing that story.

If I had been afraid of change, I would not have lived my dream of being an independent and respected woman, and it would not have been possible for my family members also eventually to live in this beautiful land of America. Yes, this journey consisted of struggles, but I was also able to see those struggles as adventures, and by going through them, I was able to become more confident in every area of life.

Life is full of risks. Sometimes our risks are scary and we have time to ponder them before we decide to take them. Other times, we discover something about ourselves because we are forced to make a split-decision about whether or not to take a risk. We might even take the risk instinctively.

Remember, without risk, there is no growth, no vitality, and no true joy.

Outweighing the Risks: Hideaki Akaiwa

When Japan was struck with a tsunami on March 11, 2011, Hideaki Akaiwa didn't think twice about taking a risk. Hideaki was at work when the earthquake and tsunami took place.

Taking a Risk in Spite of Fears

After he rushed to high ground, he immediately phoned his wife. When she didn't answer, he quickly found some scuba gear and dove into the dark, cold water, swimming hundreds of yards amid debris in his search for his wife. He finally reached the site of his home, which had been washed away, and there he found his wife struggling against the current. Fortunately, he was able to bring her to safety, but he didn't stop there. Filled with worry for his elderly mother, he waited four days, searching the official evacuation centers. Finally, he dove once more into the water that remained from the tsunami, and eventually, he found her trapped on the second floor of a neighbor's house. For Hideaki, the benefits of being reunited with his family and knowing they were safe far outweighed the risks, and if he hadn't taken those risks, he might have lost his family.

Not all of our risks are as dramatic as those that Hideaki took, but we can draw on such stories of courage to realize how precious life is and that we shouldn't waste a single moment. Better to take a risk for our benefit than to let life slip away from us.

TAKING RISKS WHEN OTHERS OPPOSE YOU: THE GRIMKE SISTERS

Sometimes taking a risk means standing up for what you believe is right when you know others will go against you.

That's what Sarah and Angelina Grimke did in the early nineteenth century in America. The sisters were born to a wealthy slave-owning family in South Carolina. Growing up on their family's plantation, they were appalled to see how African slaves were treated in the South. At that time it was illegal to teach a slave to read, but Sarah, while just a teenager, defied the law and taught her personal slave regardless. When her father found out, he was furious and threatened to whip the slave girl. Sarah then quit trying to help the slaves because she feared that helping them would just result in greater harm for them from her father and others.

Wanting to be a lawyer like her father, Sarah studied constantly at a time when women received little education. She studied secretly, and then after visiting Philadelphia and becoming introduced to Quakerism, she used religion as part of her platform to speak out about her beliefs in equality for African Americans and women. Later, her sister Angelina would join her and they would become the first female public speakers in the United States. They began to advocate for abolition of slavery, including writing tracts, despite a great deal of criticism they had to deal with. They would also become early proponents of women's rights. Thousands of people attended their lectures, and as a result, people's viewpoints in the Northern states were changed.

Taking a Risk in Spite of Fears

The Grimke sisters also knew how to practice what they preached about equality. When they found out their brother had had several illegitimate children with one of his slaves, the sisters adopted and raised the children, thereby setting an example of what true equality meant. The Grimke sisters would live to see the Civil War and the end of slavery, and although they would die before women were given the vote in the United States, their efforts helped to make it happen.

Taking a risk often means having to step out and do what you believe in even if no one else agrees with you. The Grimke sisters followed their hearts to do what they believed was right for themselves and others. In doing so, they created a better United States of America for all of us. If they could do that in a time when it was illegal to teach a slave to read and women were essentially powerless, then whatever risks you face, you can accomplish. Regardless of whether or not anyone agrees with you, you can dare to take a risk and make a better life for yourself.

DARE QUESTIONS

What risks have you taken to follow your heart?

_____
_____
_____
_____

What actions did you take?

_____
_____
_____
_____

Was your risk-taking successful? Why or why not?

_____
_____
_____
_____

What did you learn about yourself from taking those risks?

_____
_____
_____
_____

Taking a Risk in Spite of Fears

What risks are you currently facing that you need help executing in order to move forward?

_____
_____
_____

What is one thing you can do this week to help you take that risk and move forward?

_____
_____
_____
_____

PART TWO

Finding Your Place in the World

CHAPTER 4

Finding the Spirit of Adventure

"Life is either a daring adventure or nothing."
— Helen Keller

Do you want to have an adventure and experience a new world, or do you want to do the same thing you did yesterday and be restless and dissatisfied with your everyday life? Adventure can bring wondrous possibilities as you face your own uncertain and exciting future. As your life unfolds with new excitement, experiences, and adventure, you will feel alive. An adventure can change everything inside and outside of your world.

To be willing to have an adventure shows that you are open to enjoying life and believing good things will come to you. As the American author and educator Henry Van Dyke once said, "Be glad of life because it gives you the chance to love, to work, to play, and to look up at the stars."

Be willing to decide to view life as an adventure. If you can make a decision, set some goals, tap into your daring spirit, and "go for it" in an unknown world, you will be on an adventurous path. Each moment in life we are confronted with choices, small and large, that will shape what we will become. When you pause, listen to your inner daring spirit, and take the first steps on an adventurous path, everything changes.

Adventure can take you to absolutely amazing, brilliant, beautiful, and wondrous places, all freely available for you to experience. You don't have to be rich or outstanding to have an adventure. You just need to have that spirit of adventure. As Oprah Winfrey has said, "The biggest adventure you can ever take is to live the life of your dreams."

Start with your dreams. You don't need to travel to distant lands to have an adventure. You can walk to your dreams by meeting new people, having new experiences, and doing things you never thought you would do to live your dream.

Being adventurous means living life to its fullest. Dawna Markova, author of *I Will Not Die an Unlived Life*, describes her desire for an adventurous life by saying, "I will not die an unlived life. I will not live in fear of falling or catching fire. I choose to inhabit my days, to allow my living to open me, to

Finding the Spirit of Adventure

make me less afraid, more accessible, to loosen my heart until it becomes a wing, a torch, a promise."

To have a spirit of adventure means to be bold, courageous with faith, and enthusiastic. It means defining positive ways to think and behave about life and taking risks; it means going beyond the boundaries and the limitations, overcoming obstacles, and daring to be different. Anyone can have adventures. It only takes a compelling desire for life and not to be afraid of being vulnerable and open to the various forces that swirl around you.

Take this opportunity to step outside the safe "boundaries" of the past and experiment with something new. You may find that something you'd been scared of is actually a lot of fun. Go ahead, explore.

Most times, your natural versatility and boundless energy can lead you into many experiences. If there are no experiences to be enjoyed, well, you can create some! A lot of times, your restlessness will stir things up and really create some drastic change! That is okay, for the most part, as long as you don't create conflict and burn all your bridges to try and calm your restlessness. With your clear destiny, the purpose of creating change is to help you grow.

There may be times, though, when you fear change and cling with all your strength to the "old way of doing things." Well, don't! Yes, change can be frightening—even for you—but believe that adventure and change are your destiny and see yourself as the initiator of progress.

When I came to America in my twenties, not only was I on an adventure, but I knew I was an initiator of progress. I was coming to the United States to study interior design, something no other Korean woman, to my knowledge, had ever done before in the U.S. and I was seeking a new life. I put all my desires and goals into two thoughts—being an independent and respected woman and having freedom. I liked that in America everyone was treated equally and given the same opportunities, including divorced and unmarried women. Women's lives were not restricted to an armchair at home, so to speak, like they were for many women in Korea. I loved adventures, exploring everything, and creating my life in my own way with the freedom available in America. In order to fulfill my destiny, I was ready to break with tradition and expand my personal horizons. To accomplish these goals, I relied on my adventurous and enthusiastic personality. I took my life as one long non-conformist adventure in spirit. I had the audacity to believe that no matter what I decided to do, everything would work out for me.

I landed in America with one bag of clothes and the dream of becoming an "independent and respected woman." As I told you earlier, I arrived in Los Angeles, California not knowing anyone and I only had a friend in Chicago, who prearranged for me to be picked up by her friend, Miss Lee. To my surprise, Miss Lee brought with her to the airport a very nice couple so she could introduce me to them. I was going to live with them since she could not take me to her place. She had been working for a rich family for two years by contract as part of the process of getting a green card. I had no idea that she had already found me a job like hers with a very rich family who were friends of her employer. Since I had nowhere else to go, I followed Miss Lee and the nice couple to their place.

This couple lived a long way from the airport in a gated community with a few neighbors. Each family had acres of land with horses. When we got to the gate, the security guard let us in and we went to their house. I was not used to living this well. The couple welcomed me and showed me around their house. Not only did they have a large home, but they had a separate guesthouse where I would stay. It had a hexagon shape, with windows all around and beautiful scenery. That was going to be my room. I felt like Cinderella. I could get lost just walking around their estate, which included a rose garden, a herb garden, an Olympic-size swimming pool, and a horse stable. Each family member had his or her own horse. I could look up to the mountains and see the snow, then down below I could see the full blooming roses in their garden. I had never seen this phenomenal beauty in the late fall in my country. Nor had I ever seen such a rich lifestyle because after the Korean War, my country was divided, small, and poor. I thought I was in a utopia! Everything looked so beautiful and peaceful. You can see why I instantly came to love the changes I was experiencing.

The next day, my job started of babysitting the couple's two-year-old daughter. They had two children in college, one in junior high, and the two-year-old daughter. The couple was busy with social engagements quite often. The language barrier made it challenging sometimes for me to communicate with them, but I took it as a great opportunity to practice speaking English, which I'd never had an opportunity to do in Korea. At this new place, I had a hard time getting up early in the morning at first to help the lady prepare her boys' lunch and breakfast, mostly due to the time difference.

My new employers were Catholics, while I had been raised in a family that didn't practice religion. My father had grown up in an aristocratic household where he had learned about Confucius doctrine and Chinese literature as well as Korean. But my mother had sent us to church where we could learn good things, and when my sister and I were chosen to dance at the church during its Christmas and Easter programs, my mother helped us to practice and I loved participating. Now that I was in America and had a job, I began praying regularly—that I would get up on time. One morning, I woke up feeling that a hand was on my back and shaking me. It was the same way my mom used to wake me up in the morning for school. I was surprised and looked around to see my mother, but she was not there. I knew in my heart it was God's answer to my prayers. God was watching over me through my mother's prayers as well.

The first Sunday after I arrived, Miss Lee came to take me to church with Dr. Han, a dentist who was the minister's sister. When we reached the church, which was a small Korean one, I was introduced to the kind female minister. I was so happy that I could speak Korean with my new friends. It was a joy to go to church every Sunday and meet new friends, and eat Korean food, which comforted my broken and lonely heart.

After a month of living in the beautiful house with my employers, they asked me to sign a contract to work for the family for two years, and they promised to help me get a green card. It sounded like I had passed the trial period for the job, and their offer sounded very tempting. But then I started thinking about my purpose for coming to the U.S. I realized I needed to go to school to be an interior designer. I couldn't waste time in this house just for a green card. The couple was very disappointed in my decision and I knew I would miss living in the most spectacular house I had ever seen. Now, I had no clue where I would live.

I talked to Minister Lee, about needing a new place to live so I could go to school. She asked me how much money I had brought, and "Who is going to support you?" She was so shocked to find that I only had $2,000. I couldn't expect any support from home, however, because my parents had my six younger siblings to send to school; they ranged in age from elementary school to college students, and there was no free education in Korea those days. In spite of these circumstances, I knew in my heart that I would make every effort to make my dream come true. I would not disappoint my mother again.

The minister was so sympathetic about my situation and felt my courage. She placed an ad for me in the local newspaper. It stated that a female foreign student was looking for room and board with a stipend for light work after school. My minister got several calls and finally arranged for me to meet with Mrs. Donald, a wonderful woman who seemed very pleasant and kind. She was so happy to have me. Her family had immigrated to America from Europe a long time ago. Her husband was an engineer and they had three grown children who had moved out to live their own lives. Now her husband was lying in bed with bone cancer, so she needed to attend to him twenty-four hours a day.

Once I went to live with the Donalds in South Pasadena, I went to school early in the morning on the bus to L.A. and came home around 4:30 p.m. Mrs. Donald was always waiting for me with hot tea and cookies, and she had classical music ready to play as I came in because she liked music and knew that I had studied it. Mrs. Donald was always asking, "How was school today?" I remember how much I loved that time with her. It reminded me of my mother, who was so interested in our school lives. Then we would cook dinner together. Sometimes I made Korean barbecue, which Mrs. Donald loved *so much*.

After dinner, Mrs. Donald would go upstairs while I would do my homework and listen to the news on television to improve my listening skills in English. I remember how fast the news anchors talked. My life was busy and I felt grateful for everything that had happened so I could begin my new life, but in my heart, I felt lonesome for my family.

One day, Miss Lee came to visit me at the Donalds' house. She wanted to make me a pair of pants since I didn't have many clothes. As she measured my waist, she saw that I had gained some weight. I had gone from the ninety-seven pounds I had weighed when I arrived in the U.S. to 115 pounds. She and I were both shocked and I had to stop eating my favorite Neapolitan ice cream. That was my first insight about how sugar affects a person's weight.

Miss Lee and I had become good friends by this time. She was very talented and had a great heart. She could cook, sew, make people laugh with her funny jokes, and she would always help others, such as older people who were in need. Every Sunday, Dr. Han, a dentist, would pick us up for church, and after that, she would leave us at her apartment. Miss Lee cooked Korean barbecue and made instant kimchi, a spicy, fermented cabbage dish, the national dish of Korea. It was so delicious. Sundays were filled with joy and strength, Korean food and friendship, all of which helped me to go on learning new things.

During this time, I was invited to attend foreign student activities by the missionaries from Hope Church, a large American church in downtown Los Angeles. I met the most loving and kind missionary named Doris Bond. She was a devoted Christian and had lived in many other countries as a missionary. She was still single and in her fifties. Doris owned a small Volkswagen Beetle and gave me rides whenever I moved to different homes and to church. She was my guardian angel. When she found out that I was living in South Pasadena, but that my school was in Los Angeles, she introduced me to a missionary family who lived in the Hollywood area in Los Angeles and I went to stay with them.

Mrs. Donald was sad to see me leaving, but she understood how far away the school was from her home. I introduced a nice foreign student from Indonesia to Mrs. Donald. This student was a great cook and I loved her curry dish at school. Every student who lived with Mrs. Donald came to know me since she was always talking about me, and the students were always telling me that she would ask them how I was.

The new Christian family I was living with was very nice and their children were going to graduate school. The children would bring their friends home, so it was always a lively place with lots of noise. As a result, however, I decided it was better for me to study at the main library in L.A., since it was a nice, clean, and quiet place.

One summer night, I had one of the most risk-taking adventures of my life. After I had a long study session in the main library in L.A., I took a bus home as usual and got off on Hollywood Boulevard. I usually didn't come home that late at night and it was already dark out. As I was enjoying my walk home that summer night, I suddenly heard a man's voice telling me to "Come here." I looked behind me to see a young, black man trying to grab me. I was shocked. There was no one else on the street and it was dark and quiet. I ran with all my strength to Franklin Avenue. I ran through the traffic to stop him from following me. There were lots of honking noises and cars were stopping. I got to Franklin Avenue and looked for the house I had moved to a few days earlier. I couldn't find the house since all the houses looked absolutely alike and I couldn't remember the address. I ran around two blocks to find the house in the dark. I was so scared that the man might show up again.

When I was growing up in Korea, our main form of transportation was riding a bus. Everybody took a bus everywhere since people didn't own cars. Many people used to come home late before the midnight curfew. There were lots of people on the street until that time, so it was a total culture shock for me to see no one on the street since everyone was riding in a car in America. It was a miracle that night that I found the house in the midst of chaos. I was safe and I knew my mom's prayers to protect me had been answered by God.

After that incident, Doris found a new place for me in Los Angeles, close to school. I lived with Mrs. Hall, whose husband had passed away and she had no children. She was a devoted Christian and had a big, beautiful house, where she took care of three elderly ladies. She needed me on Sundays to watch the ladies and have lunch with them so she could attend church. The ladies enjoyed talking with me and eating lunch with deliciously baked chicken and soup, which Mrs. Hall had already prepared for us. All this time, I felt so blessed to have been living with wonderful people in nice places. It gave me peace of mind so I could study. It also gave me an excellent opportunity to learn the language and culture. These American people treated me with so much kindness and respect.

Between school and my jobs, I was so busy that I felt I was running around like a chicken with its head cut off. So, one day, Mrs. Hall told me that she would lend me the money for my tuition so I didn't have to run around and work so much. I was so surprised and asked, "How can I pay you back when I only have a part-time job?" She replied, "When you get a full-time job after graduation, you can pay me back." Today, I know that God's grace was working through her.

What a wonderful country America was! There were no jobs for students in Korea in those days. I was so happy to find hourly jobs through students or school in America. I enjoyed every one of the jobs that I never had a chance to do in Korea. The best job I had was working during lunch hour at the sandwich shop in Karl's Supermarket in Korea town. I was hired to work during lunch hour to get the orders for the cook since most customers were Americans, and I got a free delicious sandwich besides hourly payment. How lucky can you get! Looking back on my student days, I enjoyed every odd job and good and tough moments because I could never easily experience them in my country in those days.

I was going to school full-time and working part-time wherever I could. I really needed a car to get from place to place. My missionary friend, Doris, had an engineer friend from church, named Mr. Hepburn, and one day, he bought an old Volkswagen Beetle and fixed it up for me. It cost $800. That was big money for me in those days, but I was so excited to have it. I had to learn to drive a car with a stick shift for the first time in my life—on the freeway to Palm Springs! It was definitely an adventurous experience, and I will never forget the dreams I later had of my body flying at speeds of over sixty miles per hour.

After I got a full-time teaching job, I bought a new car, which had an automatic shift. It was too easy to drive and I missed my stick shift Volkswagen. Looking back on all these experiences, I can see how my willingness to take the adventure of coming to America to study and have faith that everything would all work out resulted in wonderful people and opportunities coming into my life to fulfill my needs.

My adventurous spirit opened a new door for me to create an exciting life, and it definitely gave me the opportunity to grow with wisdom and gratitude. Trusting God to help us with our adventure means being a co-creator with Him and having faith that everything will work out for the best, and that's exactly what happened for me on this great adventure I was open to experiencing.

Another door opened for me when my angel, Doris, introduced me to Mary, who had a beautiful house on Highland and Wilshire Blvd. in Los Angeles. While I was doing my student teaching, I had to find a new place since Mrs. Hall was retiring and selling her big house. So I rented a room from Mary that included my own living room, which had a great view of the backyard. Mary gave me a really good rent of only $100 a month. I really liked it there, but before long, Mary had to sell the house so I found an apartment that

I could afford when I got my teaching position in the Los Angeles School District.

Then one day in 1976, Mary called me to come to see her condo close to downtown Los Angeles. It was an older, but very nice, three-story brick and stone building. On the third floor, there was one unit for sale because the couple who owned it was retiring to Florida. The unit had one bedroom with a living room and all the furniture was included in the price of $7,500 they were asking for it. Since I didn't have that much money, this nice couple allowed me to make a down payment of $2,000, which I borrowed, and then I made payments, like on a loan, for over two years until it was paid off. I was really happy to have the nice furniture, and be close to my dear friend Mary, who lived on the second floor. Then three years later, I sold the condo for $35,000! Holy Cow! I learned then the power of timing in the real estate market. Now I live in the city of Santa Monica where I walk daily on the bluff overlooking the ocean, and enjoy watching the magnificent sunsets.

Most of those wonderful and kind people who were the foundation of my life in America have now passed away, except Mary, who is such a generous and kind person, and at age eighty-three, is now living in her hometown in Tennessee. I miss them all so much and regret that I didn't have time to visit them more once I left their homes. My life was incredibly busy with my full-time school and part-time workload, and most of that time, I didn't have a car so I couldn't get around so easily. I was concentrating on taking care of what was in front of me and building the future then, but I am eternally grateful for meeting those wonderful people who helped me and guided me to be who I am now in life. They are evidence to me that when you go on an Adventure with your Clear Dream and Vision, the right people will show up to help you along and ensure that you have a wonderful experience along the way.

As Janet and Chris Attwood say in their book *The Passion Test*, "When the passion is clear, the how will show up." It was amazing that once I set about fulfilling my passion to be an "independent and respected woman," how to do so showed up in my life every step of the way.

It's Never Too Late for Adventure: Jeanne Socrates' Story

Jeanne Socrates is living proof that it's never too late to take an adventure in exploring your passion. On July 8, 2013, Jeanne became the oldest woman at age seventy to sail solo around the world, after she arrived in Victoria, British Columbia's inner harbor that day.

A retired British math teacher and grandmother, Jeanne decided to pursue her new passion, and it took her three attempts to succeed. The first time engine trouble ended her effort. The second time in 2010, she was faced with a storm off Cape Horn that made her have to cancel the rest of her voyage.

But in October, 2012, she set off from Victoria, British Columbia in an eleven-meter cruiser. Acting as skipper, navigator, engineer, and chef, she spent 259 days at sea before she successfully sailed back into Victoria.

Shortly after arriving in Victoria, she described her voyage as a victory for the elderly, stating that she is the oldest by a longshot to make the voyage, and that people shouldn't think others cannot succeed because they are older. "As soon as you mention your age and number to other people, they get very ageist. They classify you and put you in a pocket as being old and no good. But we shouldn't be—we are no different as people." To me, Jeanne Socrates is living proof that it's never too late to embrace the spirit of adventure.

If you and I were not bold, being courageous enough to take adventures and risk and go beyond the boundaries, limitations, and obstacles before us, and daring to be different, where would I be, and where would you be?

Perhaps after reading about having an adventurous spirit, you feel intrigued, but you're not sure what kind of adventure you want to experience, or how to awaken your adventurous spirit. The way to cultivate an adventurous spirit is to be open to opportunities and seek out new experiences. Adventures lie all around us, even in our ordinary days. Here are some ways you could begin to cultivate your spirit of adventure:

- Take a class in something you've never tried but have always been curious about like watercolor painting, scuba diving, ballroom dancing, cooking, computers, or whatever grabs your curiosity.

- Become a lifelong learner. Take seminars, workshops, and read books about self-growth to empower you to create the life you want.

- Be curious. Try new things. Seek out information. Look up stuff you don't know and explore new ideas. Be open to wherever your adventurous spirit takes you.

- Seek out other cultures—whether it's going to a foreign film, or trying a new cuisine like Korean, Indian, or Greek, or visiting foreign countries.

- Travel new places. Take a trip to a country you always wanted to see. Explore the entire world if it's possible. If not, visit a nearby town you haven't visited before or a museum or new restaurant or any place new. Learn new things and enjoy the new sights.

- Engage in adventurous activities you love such as snorkeling, scuba diving, mountain climbing, or parasailing.

Dare Questions

What do you want to manifest so you can achieve your highest potential?

_____
_____
_____

What mindsets can you have or actions can you take to reach your highest potential?

_____
_____
_____

Make a list of all the adventures you have had in life. How did they make you feel?

_____
_____
_____
_____

How did they benefit you?

_____
_____
_____

DARING TO CHANGE

What dreams in your life are still unfulfilled?

_____
_____
_____
_____

If you could go on an adventure right now, where might it take you?

_____
_____
_____
_____

CHAPTER 5

Creating Your Vision with Intention

"A vision is more than the future as we imagine it might turn out. It is a willed future...a picture of the future as we want to make it."
— James Gregory Lord

"Where there is no vision, the people perish."
— Proverbs 29:18

Making a change will result in failure unless you have a vision of where you want to go. Now that you've cultivated your adventurous spirit and you're ready to take risks, you need a purpose, a vision to move toward so you can move forward. If you want to change your life for the better, you need a clear vision with detailed goals or action plans for what you want to accomplish.

DARING TO CHANGE

In their book *Empowerment: The Art of Creating Your Life as You Want It*, David Gershon and Gail Straub describe the importance of having a vision:

> In order to create anything, you must have a vision of what it is you want to manifest. The more definite and clear the vision, the more definite and clear the manifestation. Creating a vision for your life requires a willingness to explore and discover what's important to you, not somebody else. When you have a compelling vision, you can let go of your self-limiting beliefs easier and create what you want.

Ask yourself: What are my dreams, purposes, passions, and priorities in life? What gives my life meaning? What is possible for me? What do I value? One of the most important things you will be doing on your journey is discovering and clearly articulating a clear vision for your life.

Visualize your vision in your mind on a daily basis and daily affirm your vision out loud; then watch how your life will begin to change in response to it.

Author and motivational speaker Brian Tracy says, "The three keys to high achievement are, 'Clarity, Clarity, Clarity,' with regard to your goals. Your success in life will be largely determined by how clear you are about what it is you really, really want."

Creating Your Vision with Intention

Get clarity, think big, and be bold. In making any change in life, you need to have a defined, clear vision for what you want to accomplish. Clarity is choosing a change that you deeply desire—one that you will be inspired to work toward no matter what challenges will lie ahead. The drive for real change—the kind of change that alters the course of your life or business—comes from a deep, powerful hunger and desire to do something big and meaningful. That's the kind of change I was yearning for when I was in my twenties and came to the United States. Just like I did, you have the ability to create your life. Commit yourself to your vision emotionally, mentally, and spiritually.

Once you determine what your vision is, it's time to set intentions, which are goals along the way to achieving the bigger picture of your vision. Setting an intention is deciding to take action to bring about what you want, which is important in everything we do in life. Once you create a vision and set intentions, try not to be attached to when or how those intentions are achieved, but be clear and focused about what you want. Worrying about when it will become reality only prevents it from happening. The universe will deliver when you are open and ready to receive it. You have to believe, once you set your intention, that you are working toward it and God is co-creating with you to bring about your desire.

Marcia Wieder, the founder and CEO of Dream University, stresses the importance of setting your intention:

> Not having a clear picture of what we want is often the first obstacle in attaining our dreams. We cannot have "intent" if we don't know what we want. Simply focus on one thing as your intent; it doesn't have to be huge or far-reaching. Acknowledge that you did what you said you would and then, take the next step. By setting an intention, you make it clear to yourself and others, just what you plan to do. Setting an intention is to redefine what it means to be serious about your dreams.

In setting my own intentions, I always remember this quote from Hillel the Elder, a famous Jewish religious teacher from the first century B.C.: "If I am not for myself, then who will be for me? And if I am only for myself, then what am I? And if not now, when?" Life, after all, is made up of choices and decisions. We can't expect others to make the decisions and choices for us. We need to do it ourselves, now, and we need to trust that what we do for ourselves will ultimately be for the good of others as well.

When your intention is clear, it will begin to appear. That's exactly what happened to me when I came to the United States. I had come with the intention to be an "independent and respected woman" and to study interior design. But it

Creating Your Vision with Intention

never hurts to keep clarifying your intention as I did when I arrived in the United States. I'll go into the details of that later when I talk about synchronicity, but ultimately, I changed my intention to becoming a teacher.

In the end, I earned my master's degree in education with a teaching credential, and I got a job offer at the Los Angeles School District in 1974. I, as a foreign student, never ever thought it was possible for me to be offered a teaching position in the U.S. in those days, but the school district sponsored me so I could change my student visa status to that of a permanent resident. I received a work permit first and later I got a green card.

For me, becoming a teacher in Los Angeles was a miraculous event. I had never imagined that a poor student from Korea would have a teaching opportunity and be a permanent resident in the U.S. When it happened, it proved to me that when you have a compelling dream, a clear vision, and the courage to pursue your dream, then no matter what, God helps you to co-create your destiny.

My point is that if I had not had a big compelling dream in my heart, I never would have had the courage to get on the plane that brought me to the United States. When you have a big dream and clear vision and you take action on it with all your heart, the how will show up to guide you through.

Edison had a clear intention and vision when he was trying to invent the lightbulb. He failed 10,000 times but his intention was clear. He viewed every failure as bringing him one step closer to success because he had learned one more way that would not work so he could figure out what would work. In the end, he was successful in inventing the lightbulb as well as many other inventions, including the phonograph and an early motion picture camera. He made incredible contributions for the benefit of all humanity. It was his vision that led to his success because he held onto it even when he experienced failure until he finally succeeded.

EXERCISE: DETERMINING YOUR VISION

To create a vision for yourself, ask yourself the following questions:

Where would I like to be next month?

_____
_____
_____

In six months?

_____
_____
_____

Creating Your Vision with Intention

Next year?

_____
_____
_____

In five years?

_____
_____
_____

How do I want to feel about myself?

_____
_____
_____

What do I want to do with the rest of my life?

_____
_____
_____

What is my true passion?

_____
_____
_____

Create a vision for yourself by asking yourself all of the above questions. Most importantly, write down your answers. State your goals clearly on paper and put them where you can see them every day so they will sink into your mind and you will work daily toward achieving them.

In order to manifest your vision, you also may use the following techniques daily:

Affirmations: An affirmation is a simple statement affirming what you want in your life *as if it already exists*. Examples include:

- I am having (instead of "I will have") an amazing career.
- I am making (instead of "plan to make") enough money every year to take a relaxing two-week vacation.
- I trust that change brings good things and help us grow.
- I succeed in whatever I put my mind to.
- I have perfect health and a radiant body.
- My needs are easily met in the world of abundance.
- I am happy, healthy, and living my dream.
- I am flowing with life easily and effortlessly.

Creating Your Vision with Intention

TO CREATE AN AFFIRMATION:

1. Be concrete: Write it down. Then say it, see it, and read it.
2. Be succinct so you can focus on it easily. Instead of cramming several related issues into one statement, separate them into different statements.
3. Be specific to create clear results. State all the details you want and when you want it to manifest. "I have a great new job in the financial sector; I am making $100,000 a year by September 15, 2014."
4. Be positive about creating something, instead of overcoming problems. You need to affirm the end result for what you want. Instead of "I am going to lose weight," write down "I am slim, healthy, and fit."
5. Review your affirmations daily and update them on a regular basis.

VISUALIZATION:

Visualization is the mental image or picture of what you want to create in your life. You can use the affirmation and visualization together consistently for the best results. As you speak the affirmation, visualize images that you want to create as if they were part of a movie. You should be the star in that movie. By creating this movie or vision in your subconscious mind, you change the outer life, your reality.

Vision Board

Here's an idea to help make your visions more real and obtainable. Create a Vision Board, sometimes called a Visual Explorer or Creativity Collage, which is a set of pictures from various magazines, or you can draw images that represent your visions.

Your visions will give your life purpose and direction. Your vision board is a picture of what your future will look like according to what you desire. Remember the old saying, "Don't die with your music still inside you." Your vision board should be a trigger that helps you visualize your life as you want it to be. You can draw your own or cut out the pictures for your vision from magazines or find images on websites that you can use.

Nobody succeeds without first having a vision of what he or she wants. Even when people say to themselves that the vision can't become a reality, true visionaries hold onto their visions and the spirit of adventure that must come with them. Visionaries take the risks necessary to create the changes in their lives and in the world that they want. And stories of the successes of these visionaries are abundant. Following are just a couple of stories of such visionaries who succeeded:

Having the "Wright" Vision: The Wright Brothers

Everyone knows the Wright brothers made the first successful flight on December 17, 1903, in Kitty Hawk, North Carolina. But did you know that at the time they were bicycle mechanics? They knew nothing about how to build a plane or make it fly, but they had a clear vision and set their intention for what they wanted.

When the Wright Brothers were little, they enjoyed playing with paper airplanes. When they saw a big hawk flying freely in the sky, they dreamt about what it would be like to fly like a bird. Often they made themselves paper wings and then went up a hill and jumped off, trying to fly. Of course, they ended up rolling down the hill and scratching themselves all over. But their dreams remained strong, and after endless research and failures over the years, eventually they made that historic flight by airplane at Kitty Hawk, and ever since then, travel has never been the same.

The Wright Brothers had the "Wright" vision—one based in strong intentions, believing in themselves, and taking actions to make their dreams come true.

DARING TO CHANGE

THE WILL TO DO IT: JOHN F. KENNEDY

In May 1961, United States President John F. Kennedy proclaimed that it would be a national goal to land a man on the moon and return him safely to earth and that it would be achieved before the end of that decade. This goal was astounding to people who heard Kennedy's intent, but it set the stage for incredible growth in the nation's emerging space program. Of course, Kennedy knew that putting a man on the moon was no small task. When he asked rocket scientist Dr. Werner von Braun, "What will it take to build a rocket that will carry a man to the moon and safely bring him back to earth?" Dr. Von Braun answered with just five simple words, "The will to do it."

Kennedy and all of the space program's team set an intention and then took action to make it happen. During this time, a tragic turn of events happened on November 29, 1963. The president who set the moon as NASA's goal was assassinated, but that could not kill the dream the president had set.

This goal was also fueled by competition with the Soviet Union, a competition dubbed as the "space race." It resulted in the Kennedy Space Center transforming from a testing ground for new rockets into a launch pad for a human to go to the moon, and by the end of that decade, and within the timeframe of the goal, it was achieved.

Creating Your Vision with Intention

Apollo 11 was launched in 1969. The eight-day mission took the crew on a 935,000 mile round-trip journey to the moon, and on July 20th of that year, an estimated 530 million people watched the televised image and heard Neil Armstrong's words as he became the first human to set foot on the moon. His "one small step" made a goal that had seemed like science fiction into a reality, thereby fulfilling President Kennedy's vision. Without the vision, landing on the moon would have remained a distant dream.

Dare Questions

What is your vision for your life?

_____
_____
_____

If you haven't already, write down your affirmations for your new vision of your life:

_____
_____
_____

What are you willing to do to make your vision into a reality?

_____
_____
_____

What can you add to your vision to make it even more remarkable and desirable for you? Don't limit yourself to thinking your full vision isn't possible when you answer this question.

_____
_____
_____

CHAPTER 6

Overcoming Obstacles and Adversities

"Things you want are always possible; it is just that the way to get them is not always apparent. The only real obstacle in your path to a fulfilling life is you, and that can be a considerable obstacle because you carry the baggage of insecurities and past experiences."
— Les Brown

No great accomplishment can take place without first overcoming obstacles. So once you have your vision and set your intention to make it a reality, it's important for you to stick with your own path and trust in yourself and your intuition *in spite* of the obstacles that may litter the way. And with every obstacle defeated, you grow a little stronger. Once you overcome your obstacles through hard work, the doors to success open and the rewards of right living fall into your lap.

Victor Henson, a famous German zoologist and the father of ocean biology, said, "Don't wait until everything is just right. It will never be perfect. There will always be challenges, obstacles, and less than perfect conditions. So what! Get started now. With each step you take, you will grow stronger and stronger, more and more skilled, more and more self-confident, and more and more successful."

Perhaps like me, you began your career early in life to support yourself; if you went to college, you probably worked part-time during your school years, and full-time over the summer. Even though you began working at an early age, you've likely frequently had to struggle in the workplace. You've probably been through power struggles, layoffs, firings, and demotions during your career. But the early struggles in your job *will* lead to growth and better things down the road. You need to go beyond your circumstances and be ready for the challenges.

Life's challenges aren't necessarily battles. Instead, we can choose to look at them as lessons that give us the opportunity to improve. You also need to use the gift of progressive, forward thinking, at times. Sometimes problems need to be approached in an unusual way—flexibility and adaptability

Overcoming Obstacles and Adversities

can help us to solve them. We can refuse to see only black and white or limited choices. We can think outside the box to find other possibilities for getting around a problem or achieving a goal or desire.

When I came to the U.S. in my twenties, after college, I had a broken heart from my divorce, and only $2,000 to support myself or pay for school. I was not fluent in English, and I didn't know anyone in Los Angeles. I could have used all of these circumstances as reasons why I could have doubted my chance of success. Instead, I chose to believe in my dream and completely devoted myself to making it a reality. I chose to see my cup as "half-full," not "half-empty." Just like I did, you can choose to live beyond your circumstances if you dare to change how you see things, to create and believe in your vision, and to focus on what you need to do to get there. As author Benjamin Disraeli said, "Man is not the creature of circumstances; circumstances are the creatures of man." If you truly want something, you can find a way to have it in spite of obstacles and circumstances.

Although it felt like a miraculous event to me when I was offered a teaching position from a public school in the L.A. School District, it really was the result of how I had set my intention. I had wanted to learn the American educational system as a volunteer before I returned home during my last semester of graduate school. This vision manifested itself into something even better—a job. It was my first teaching position and the school, Hobart Blvd. Elementary, was one of the area's largest elementary schools in the district, with 2,400 students and over 200 staff members on the mid-west side of Los Angeles.

I was assigned to a combination kindergarten through first grade class because its teacher had left after only two months of teaching. This class was composed of thirty-three students with multilingual and multicultural backgrounds. The kids were more interested in playing than learning so they didn't always pay attention to me. It was tough for me as a brand new teacher to work with a majority of the students since so many spoke Spanish while others spoke Korean and there were a few English-speaking students. My principal, Mr. Howell, would stop by to observe the classroom, and he ended up taking some of the behavior problem kids to other, more experienced teachers' classrooms. He also suggested several good ideas that helped me, and I really appreciated his attention to me as a brand new teacher.

I had to work late every night and on weekends to prepare lessons according to the students' abilities, grading their work, creating lesson plans, and providing a good learning environment with visual bulletin boards on the classroom

Overcoming Obstacles and Adversities

walls. I had such a total devotion to teaching my students that I never missed a day of work for five years until one day when my next-door teacher told me I should stay home when I had a cold so the children would not catch it. In Korea, it was a rule to go to school no matter what; having perfect attendance was very important, and we would get Perfect Attendance Awards that always meant a lot to us. But now as a teacher, I understood that staying home was best for the children if I were sick.

Besides having to adjust to these different customs in the United States, it was taking me time to master English. After just over three years of studying in the U.S., I was now an elementary school teacher in a public school so I had to teach all the subjects daily, preparing lessons and materials according to my students' ability. Everything took longer for me than the other teachers because English was my second language. As a result, many times I only slept four to five hours after preparing all the lessons and materials. I was so stressed out as a new teacher that I got shingles, which caused enormous pain in my spine. Fortunately, I was able to get rid of the pain by getting a shot in my spine. It was so painful that I never wanted to go through that again.

However, because of the obstacles I faced, I was willing to work harder and longer to improve my teaching skills, and I was resourceful. Making lesson plans trained me to organize my thoughts and information. I also learned how to present my lessons in an interesting way so they would be effective for the students.

I had great training from my master teacher, Lulu, who was an excellent primary grade teacher for my student teacher training. She had over thirty first grade children in her class, and she divided the students into a three-group teaching organization that worked beautifully. The first group would receive direct teaching from the teacher. The second group would work at the follow-up center with questions on worksheets. Then the third group would work at the learning center independently with games she made from the lesson. Lulu provided well-prepared lessons, materials, and discipline for young children to follow. Every student enjoyed learning without creating a chaos.

The room's environment reflected the theme of the lessons that Lulu was teaching. There was no struggling for control of the classroom. I was so lucky to have a great master teacher like her. She saved me from all the common headaches of not knowing how to control a class well because of the great training I received from this excellent master teacher.

As a result, I did so well running my classroom with my thirty-three first graders that my principal asked me to be a

Overcoming Obstacles and Adversities

first grade department chair, but at the time, I felt I couldn't afford to add more stress to my life by dealing with the different personalities of the teachers, so I decided to decline and concentrate on my classroom teaching. I would have many more opportunities in my career later on.

I realized deep in my heart that I had what it takes to persevere. I could face and overcome obstacles and adversities. I had survived supporting myself through school in the U.S., I had been teaching in the public schools for five years in multilingual classrooms, and I knew whatever challenge next came my way, I could succeed at it. After all, I affirmed to myself, I am a courageous, dynamic, creative, and audacious woman who can live my dream powerfully and create the life I want.

Like me, many other people have learned to live outside the box, accepting and overcoming the difficulties and challenges that come to them, so they can succeed. Let me share with you a few of their incredible stories.

FROM DARKNESS TO LIGHT: KIM WICKES

Kim Wickes has known what it is to overcome adversity, including being blind and faced with the turmoil of war. She was just a child during the Korean War. When a bomber flew over her village in rural South Korea, Kim's father told the family to lie on the ground and cover their faces, but young Kim looked up just as the bomb exploded. While she survived the bombing itself, after that, she could only see shadows and faint outlines of people or objects.

As the war continued, her family was forced to become refugees. At one point, conditions became so bad that Kim's father wanted them all to die because he felt life was no longer worth living. He contemplated ways of killing the children so they would not have to suffer. When Kim's mother refused to let them be run over by a truck, he threw his daughters into the river. Kim's mother managed to force him to go into the river to retrieve them, but Kim's baby sister was washed away and lost forever. Kim would later feel that God had saved her that day because He had a plan for her life.

Finally, Kim's mother had had enough of her father, and she thought they could better survive by splitting up. Kim went with her father, but after a while, he decided to place her in an orphanage for the deaf and blind; at the time, blindness was considered a disgrace in Korean society so he did not want to deal with Kim's disability. Eventually, Kim was moved to another orphanage where the teachers told her she would need surgery to remove one of her eyes; however, the doctors then decided to remove both of her eyes, leaving Kim

Overcoming Obstacles and Adversities

in complete darkness, no longer even being able to see the faint shadows she had seen before.

Despite these devastating occurrences, Kim was supported by teachers who encouraged her not only to read Braille but to memorize great amounts of Scripture from the Bible. Then, when the war ended, Americans began to adopt Korean children, and Kim was among the fortunate. The Wickes family of Indiana adopted her and she took their last name. Once Kim arrived in the United States, she learned English, and despite her blindness, she attended the public schools.

Already feeling blessed despite her obstacles, Kim was fortunate enough to hear Billy Graham preach when he came to Indianapolis when she was twelve. Because she was a girl and boys were treasured in Korean culture, she had always felt unworthy, but that night at the Billy Graham Crusade, she experienced Jesus enter her life. Kim then realized that she was not unworthy because Jesus could use her to show His greatness. Later, when she was sixteen, Kim heard World Vision founder Bob Pierce speak at a Youth for Christ International Conference; it was then she decided she would dedicate her life to Christian service. She went on to college, intending to become a missionary and travel the world, telling people what Jesus had done in her life.

But God had other plans for her. When she was interviewed by a reporter from a Korean newspaper about being adopted, her father read the story and wrote to her, asking her to come visit him. Kim didn't know how she could get to Korea, but she had been awarded a Fulbright scholarship to study in Vienna. While she was in Vienna, she met the U.S. Ambassador to Austria and she told him her story, including that her father wanted her to visit him. The ambassador offered to pay for her visit to South Korea, and Kim gratefully accepted. But first, she had to sing in Switzerland at the International World Conference on Evangelization, which launched her music ministry—she would go on to be a music minister for the rest of her life, including singing at many of Billy Graham's events.

With more help along the way from others interested in her story, Kim was able to reconnect with her father during a month long visit to Korea that included her performing in many concerts. During this time, Kim's father told her he had no regrets about how her life had turned out, and she confirmed that she always felt, despite everything she had undergone, that God had been watching over her.

Kim Wickes has gone on to spend her life in music ministry through her local church and at schools for the blind and at military events. In 2012, when she was interviewed

Overcoming Obstacles and Adversities

by *Decision* magazine, she said, "I've held hands with dying veterans who had nobody else to hold their hands. I've sung at a lot of military bases. The servicemen get excited to see how God can use anybody, and I always thank them for their service. Even though losing sight during the war was bad in itself, it has turned into a channel of gratitude—and God has blessed others."

Kim Wickes learned how to turn her adversity into a blessing and to use it to benefit others. Even though being blind was an obstacle, she never let it stop her. She could not remove it, but she could remove her opposition to it and find God's love and spread that to others as a result. Perhaps you can't always overcome an obstacle, but you can learn to be grateful for life regardless and find ways to make a difference in the world, or as Kim Wickes would say, "I will make darkness light."

The Hand of God: Paull Shin

Paull Shin, or Ho Bum Shin, was born in 1935 in Korea. When he was a baby, his mother became sick with breast cancer. Since she couldn't take care of her baby and his father was always away working, Paull was sent to be cared for by his grandmother.

His grandmother's household was already full. Besides Paull's grandmother, there was his uncle, his uncle's wife, and their three children. His grandmother helped to take care of all the children. Paull knew he was an unwanted addition. When Paull was six years old, his aunt beat him until his body was black and blue because he had taken some food from her own children.

Paull then decided to run away from home, thinking he would find a way to make money so he could buy his own rice cakes to eat. He stowed away on a train to Seoul, but when he arrived there, he could find no work or assistance from anyone and became a homeless street beggar. For the next two years, he slept on cold cement against the sides of buildings. When he lost his only other beggar friend, he was so lonely that he went back to his grandmother.

This time, Paull's father took him in to live with him. By then, Paull's father had remarried so Paull had to live with his stepmother and five stepchildren in one single room. Before long, Paull again left home and became a beggar on the streets of Seoul.

The Korean War exploded on June 25, 1950. Paull was fifteen years old when the U.S. Army entered Seoul. The U.S. Army Corps of Engineers was building a temporary bridge over the Han River to transport troops into Seoul and beyond. Paull daily went out to beg sweets from the soldiers, who would toss chocolate, gum, and other snacks to the children. Paull

Overcoming Obstacles and Adversities

was just one of many who followed the army trucks looking for goodies.

But one day, a soldier extended a hand to Paull, and Paull reached out, expecting to receive sweets. Instead, the soldier gripped his hand and pulled him into a truck. Because of Paull's dirty clothes, it was obvious to the soldier that the boy had nowhere to call home. With that soldier's help, Paull got to work at the U.S. Army office. He compared that soldier's hand to the hand of God, offering him a whole new life.

The soldier was a captain in the army, and when the war was over, he adopted Paull and brought him home to the United States. Paull had received no formal education in Korea, so now he began from the beginning by learning his ABC's. In time, he passed the GED test, the equivalent of earning a high school diploma and he went on to earn a Ph.D. Because of the blessings Paull received in the United States, he wanted to become a public servant to his adopted country. In time, he became a professor, a businessman, and an elected official, serving in both the Washington State House of Representatives and the Washington State Senate. He also was able in time to bring his father, stepmother, and stepbrothers to America, and he and his wife have adopted two children from Korea.

DARING TO CHANGE

As you have witnessed through these stories, you have the power to create anything you want in life. By developing incredible willpower, based on your passion, and by setting clear intentions, you can create a winning formula to improve your life now and for your future. Yes, there will be obstacles to overcome, but by never giving up, you will succeed.

Overcoming Obstacles and Adversities

DARE QUESTIONS

What obstacles do you feel are keeping you right now from changing your life?

_____
_____
_____
_____

What would you do with your life if these obstacles weren't in your way?

_____
_____
_____
_____

What is one thing you can do today to work toward removing these obstacles that are interfering with your dream?

_____
_____
_____
_____

PART THREE

Miracles Do Happen

CHAPTER 7

Unfolding Your Destiny with Synchronicity

"We do not create our destiny; we participate in its unfolding. Synchronicity works as a catalyst toward the working out of that destiny."
— David Richo, *The Power of Coincidence*

When we set our intention and trust that what we want will happen, God co-creates with us. When seeming coincidences happen that help to move us toward our goal, they are a sign that God or the universe is working to help us. Synchronicity happens when everything seems to be coming together perfectly to get us to where we want to be. It's when events happen just in time and on the spur of the moment to help along our personal evolution.

The famous Swiss psychologist Carl Jung was the first to use the term synchronicity to describe those moments of meaningful coincidence. Synchronicity takes the events in space and time and shows they have meaning beyond being mere chance.

In her book, *The Purpose of Your Life*, Carol Adrienne states, "Synchronicities are forces that come together in time and space, providing just what is needed. The occurrence strikes the participants as special, unexpected, or unexplainable by normal cause-and-effect rationales. The effect of a synchronicity on the psyche is to trigger awareness that maybe a great—or even a divine—purpose is at work."

When synchronicity happens, it's a reminder to us that the universe has a purpose—to help bring about what will benefit us. It is co-creation at its best, a sign that God or the universe is looking out for us. Nor do we need to interfere with the process. When we set our intentions and believe something can happen, we can't focus our energy on trying to force it to happen; that's a sign that we distrust the universe or that our ego thinks we have to do it all. Synchronicity has a supernatural way about it. It works in mysterious ways we cannot understand. We can only be delighted and appreciate the results.

My life in the United States started with many synchronicities. After arriving in California, I soon changed my intention to study interior design because I found out it was expensive to buy all the required materials, in addition to paying for my tuition, and I did not have sufficient funds. Not knowing what to do, I called my mom to ask her for advice. She didn't know much about interior design since it was so new in Korea at the time. So she suggested, "Why don't you become a professor who could earn the most respect as a woman in Korean tradition." I thought that was aligned with my desire to be a respected and independent woman. So I enrolled myself in the graduate school program, majoring in special education, which was a new field in Korea at that time as well. As I was finally finishing up my graduate degree in education, I couldn't wait to go home since it had been more than three years since I had left.

One day a thought came to me that I should visit an elementary school to see the American educational system at work before I went back home. I found a large elementary school in mid-town Los Angeles on Olympic Blvd. that had a few newly arrived Korean students. I decided to volunteer at the school in the fifth grade classroom. Because that time period was when Korean immigrants were first coming to Los Angeles in large numbers, the teachers and students really needed my help. One day, the principal asked me to come to see him. He asked me about my credentials and whether I was interested in working as a bilingual teacher at the school.

Wow! I couldn't believe what I was hearing. I never thought that I could become a teacher in the United States since I was a foreign student. I asked him, "Can I teach at the school <u>with</u> a student visa?" He wasn't sure so he told me to go to an immigration attorney to ask about the situation.

I found an American immigration attorney and went to see him. He asked me what my salary would be at the school. I had no idea. He said that he would pay me more if I would work for him. Holy cow! Can you believe that? Here I was a poor student, and now I suddenly had two job offers before I had even graduated. I was so excited that I called my mom right away and told her that I got two job offers. She was very happy and told me I should be a teacher because I would get more respect than working in an attorney's office.

In the olden days, teachers in Korea were so well-respected and honored that students wouldn't even step on the shadow of the teacher. That was the kind of teaching my mother grew up with. Thinking back, I now wonder whether if I had worked for the attorney, I would have become motivated to be an attorney. After all, I can remember my college friend in Korea telling me that I talked like a lawyer when I debated my options before making a choice.

My plan was to visit home after my last class ended that summer. But getting hired to teach at the elementary school beginning in September meant I couldn't go home until the following summer. I was so disappointed. I really wanted to see my family. When I talked to my supervisor at the college about the situation, she advised me to visit my family as I had planned. She said I could find a job any time, but seeing my family, who had been waiting for several years, was special. That was the wisest and most thoughtful advice I could receive. When I talked to the principal about the plan, he understood, but the school year began in September and he needed a teacher right away, so I wouldn't be able to take the position.

I had a heartfelt visit with my family and friends in South Korea, and then I came back to Los Angeles. About two weeks after my return in November, I received a phone call from the principal. I was surprised to hear from him. He asked me whether I still wanted to teach at his school. I was so astonished and asked him, "Didn't you hire a teacher?" He said he had hired a Chinese-American teacher, but she didn't like teaching that much because she needed to deal with so many discipline problems with the kids, so she had left to take an art director position at a recreation center. Here was that same position opened up for me again! I was obviously meant to be a teacher, helping to empower young souls. I felt I was the luckiest person alive because I was about to live my dream of being a respected and independent woman!

In order to hire me, the principal had to put an ad in the *Los Angeles Times* for a teacher position. He used his own money for it. Later, he told me that over ten people had applied from all over the United States, and he had interviewed them on the phone, but he still chose me. The school district sponsored my work visa and later I received a green card. I became the first Korean bilingual elementary school teacher in the Los Angeles School District in November, 1974. Miraculous synchronicity had been unfolding to bring about my purpose. The principal, Mr. Howell, is now ninety years old. We still have breakfast from time to time to visit with each other.

Then in September, 1984, I became a citizen of the United States, and later, I invited all of my family to celebrate and have a reunion in America. Today, they all enjoy living and being good citizens in the beautiful country of America.

As you can see, the doors open for you even when you have no connections with people who can help you. You just need to be clear about your vision and intentions and do your best with all your heart. The opportunities will always come through.

Being hired for a teaching position wasn't my first experience with synchronicity. When the Korean War began, I was a child who hadn't even started school yet. I now want to tell you how the war affected my family. This story is another example of how synchronicity worked in my life and how it can work in yours.

Miraculous Synchronicity:
My Korean War Story

When the Korean War exploded on June 25th of 1950, North Korea invaded South Korea with a declaration of war to unify Korea under communism. We needed to leave home as soon as possible, so our family went to Seoul Train Station to get on, but the train was already packed with too many people. So my mother paid for a wagon to take us to Anyang city, which was about thirteen miles south of Seoul. My father had to leave before us so he would not be caught and forced to serve in the North Korean Army. Right after we left Seoul, the Han River Bridge was bombed to prevent further members of the North Korean Army from crossing it.

A week later, the United Nations placed the forces of twenty-two member nations under U.S. command with General Douglas MacArthur as their supreme commander. The U.S. soldiers came to set up a defense barricade to prevent the Communists from coming further south.

The U.S. soldiers, however, also took advantage of women, young and old, to satisfy their sexual appetites. They were searching for women in every house in the village. To protect herself, my mother put an old towel on her hair and ashes on her face to look old. Then she hid inside the big empty house we had found to live in since people had already abandoned their homes. My sister and I then stood by the gate to the house so we could watch for the soldiers.

One day, I saw a U.S. soldier coming toward our house. I ran to my mother and told her that a soldier was coming. We were so shocked that we didn't know what to do. My mother found a tall rolled up straw mat standing in the corner by the big solid wooden entrance gate, so she hid inside the standing straw mat with my baby brother on her back. The soldier came in and looked everywhere in the house and then he finally left. I couldn't breathe during those anxious moments. I was so afraid my baby brother might cry and reveal their hiding place, but miraculously, he stayed quiet; perhaps he was sleeping or exhausted with malnutrition. Those were the longest, most anxious moments I have ever had to face.

On October 19th, the North Korean capital of Pyongyang was occupied by the U.S. Army. We were living in Anyang city for a while, then came back home when the communists retreated from South Korea. Then the North Korean Army came back down to South Korea. The Chinese communists joined with the North Koreans to launch a successful counterattack on January 4, 1951. The communists again advanced into the south, recapturing Seoul, the South Korean capital.

In the freezing, icy cold winter, my mother again took me and my younger sister with her while she carried my baby brother on her back. Not knowing what lay ahead, we started our journey on foot to the city of Anyang where we stayed for a while until the North Korean soldiers, plus Chinese communist soldiers, approached it. From there we fled to Suwon City, twenty-one miles from Seoul city. Now my mother decided to go to Inchon City where the military police were residing at that time. It was much more secure there, she thought. The city of Inchon was so overcrowded with refugees that we spent hours looking for a room. Finally, my mom found us a small room that we could share with other people since rooms were so hard to come by. My mother didn't have any money because her bundle of expensive clothes was stolen from her during the journey by a young woman who had offered to help carry them.

The government was giving out rice to refugees, so my mother received the rice and then went to the rice cake factory so she could make rice cakes. Then she sold the rice cakes on the street to make money for us to live on. She was a young mother in her twenties who had never had to sell anything on the street until then. My mother decided to disguise herself to look older; she didn't want the soldiers to try to take advantage of her, and she didn't want anyone to recognize her at the market. So my young mother put ashes on her face and wore an old towel on her head. She probably felt embarrassed by this situation of selling goods on the street, so she asked me to stay with the rice cakes on the street while she stood nearby. However, every time someone came to buy a rice cake, I didn't know how to give change back to the person. I hadn't learned math yet. So I was calling, "Mom, help!" She ran to me, saying, "Shh!" with embarrassment, and then she took care of selling the cake and giving the change.

One day, my mother was walking through the market on the street when she saw some clothes for sale that looked familiar. She was surprised to find the woman who had stolen her clothes selling them on the street! Mother went to take all of her clothes back, but the woman had already sold a few of the good ones. My mother took whatever was left for us so we would have some valuables to sell if needed.

A few days later while we were selling rice cakes, a policeman came by who kept looking at my mother. He walked away, but then he came back to look at her again and finally asked her, "Do you have a brother living in Kang Nung province?" Mother said, "Yes." The policeman turned out to be my uncle's good friend who was on a business trip to Inchon as a policeman. Both my mother and he were shocked to run into each other in the refugee city of Inchon. They were overjoyed by this reunion. He immediately bought all the rice cakes we were selling and gave us 7,000 Won, which he had in his pocket at that time, and he gave my mother the news about her brother. My mom was filled with joy to hear that her brother and his family were safe.

This brother, my uncle, had raised my mom and he was living in their birthplace in Kang Nung City along the East Coast by the sea. As soon as he had heard that the North Korean army had invaded Seoul, he had left in a truck through Dai Kwal Lyung, a long, long mountain road by the East coast, to rescue us and take us to Kang Nung. While he was driving on the mountain road, North Korean soldiers began shooting at vehicles. My uncle had to run away so he couldn't reach Seoul to rescue us. My mother and all of us were touched to hear how worried my uncle had been. We were grateful to know that he loved us so much that he had tried to save us in the middle of the war. How many other people would have done that? Such action takes absolute courage and love, and today, I still miss him so much since he has passed away.

Fortunately, now my uncle's friend could let him know we were okay. That's how we met my uncle's good friend and received God's blessings through him during the chaos of the war. What a miraculous synchronicity that was! It reminds me of what the author Deepak Chopra said, that "synchronicity is coincidence from God's blessings."

At that time, we still hadn't heard from or found my father. My mother still wanted to find us a room of our own so we were visiting many houses in Inchon city. The next day, she went to look at another house and there was my father. Isn't that a miracle? He had managed to run away from Seoul to the province of Chung Cheong where he had grown up. Then he heard we had gone to Anyang, but by the time he reached where we were living, most of the houses were burnt and destroyed—only a few houses were left standing, so he had come to Inchon. We had all come to the same city, but we didn't know it and it had taken a while to find each other because the city was overflowing with so many refugees. It was a miracle that we had found each other in the city packed with people. What a miraculous synchronicity we experienced in the unfolding of our destiny!

DARE QUESTIONS

Have you ever experienced synchronicity in your life?

_____
_____
_____

Have you ever felt that you just knew something would turn out the way you wanted it to and it did?

_____
_____
_____

Have you ever wanted something to happen that didn't? Were you worried about it? Do you think maybe worrying rather than trusting could be a part of why the synchronicity didn't happen for you?

_____
_____
_____
_____
_____

CHAPTER 8

Moving Mountains to Make It Happen

"I do not think there is any other quality so essential to success of any kind as the quality of perseverance. It overcomes almost everything, even nature."
— John D. Rockefeller

Nothing can be achieved in life without perseverance. Once you have your vision and you believe through synchronicity that all the pieces will come together to make it happen, you also have to be prepared to do your part. That's where perseverance comes in. It's always possible that obstacles will arise to get in your way, but you can persevere by understanding that obstacles just help to clarify your vision and prepare it to become reality when the time is right. We can't control how and when things will happen, but we can always persevere in our belief that they will happen, and we can do what we can to help bring them about. As an old song says, "Even a miracle needs a hand."

Giving up on something in life is always the easiest route, but it is not the route to success. When you are trying to potty-train your children, all of your efforts may fail repeatedly, but that doesn't mean you give up. We all have projects that seem too big, too difficult, or too impossible. But if we can persevere, all those projects will be a success.

When I was offered a teaching job in the Los Angeles School District as a Korean bilingual teacher in the multilingual (Spanish, Vietnamese, Korean, and English speaking) elementary school, I was excited, but it also was hard work that required individualized lesson plans, discipline, motivation, and good planning. In the classroom, teaching happens through talking. I had to use English, a language in which I was still not overly fluent yet, so sometimes I thought to myself, "Why am I doing what I am doing?!" But I stuck to the teaching position to fulfill my mantra to be an "independent and respected woman."

I loved my first grade students who were so mischievous but forgiving. No matter how many times I stopped them from playing their favorite games because they did not do their homework, or I had to bench them for fighting in the schoolyard, the next day, they would always smile or say nice things about my hair or my dress as if they had forgotten all about the punishment. I wish grown-ups could act the same way as young kids in forgiving others.

I chose to persevere, regardless, and I soon discovered that God had purposely given me this opportunity because so many Korean students were coming into the school district. A large influx of Korean immigrants were arriving in Los Angeles in the 1970s and their children needed to be taught. As a result, American teachers needed more understanding about Korean language, culture, and family values.

The teachers' main complaints were, "The Korean students are not looking at me when I talk to them." This was a misunderstanding coming from cultural differences. What about eye contact? When talking to older people, Korean children may not look straight into their eyes; instead, the children may hold their eyes and heads down to show "respect." So frustrated teachers kept asking students to look at their eyes, and students got frustrated and put their eyes lower than the teacher's eyes. They did not understand English well or the cultural differences. To help with these issues, I offered many parent education classes at school and in the community, and parent conferences in the region.

Then I decided to offer Korean language and culture classes for district teachers who were required to take multicultural education. I was also invited as a speaker at the California bilingual and bicultural conferences, and my class was an exemplary bilingual class used as a model for advisors from the state department and educators in other school districts. As Korean bilingual classes grew, more materials were needed, so I applied for and received a mini-grant from the Region Office in the district to write Korean reading materials with diagnostic tests for classroom use.

In 1983, I was invited to be the First Principal at the Saturday School of Korean Language and Culture Education for the second generation of Koreans in Glendale city, adjacent to Los Angeles, where the Korean population was growing. This program was designed to teach second generation Koreans about their mother language and culture, history, and customs so they would understand their roots, have pride in their heritage, and become bilingual citizens, so they could be more productive and successful citizens in society.

During that time in 1984, I campaigned with Korean language school board members to amend the State Education Code for credit for the Korean Language as a Second Language for High School Graduation. When this amendment was granted, it became a great benefit for high school students when applying to college. Around that time, the Korean Institute of S. California wanted to open a private elementary school from K-6th grades. Again I was in charge of the project working with the Los Angeles School District and California State

Education Department. As a result, in 1985, the first private elementary school was opened by the Korean community. Today Korean Institute of S. California has twelve branch schools in surrounding cities where the large Korean population resides. It offers Korean language and culture education to students from K through 12th grades. At the fortieth anniversary of the Korean Institute of S. California in 2012, I became a recipient of the Achievement Award from the Korean Institute of S. California for my many contributions to the Korean Institute.

Nor was that the end of everything I was involved in. In the 1970s, the Los Angeles School District received a Title VII grant from the Federal Government to implement a bilingual program, since 70 percent of the school district's student population consisted of minority children in need of bilingual support. The principal needed a Bilingual Program Coordinator to implement and oversee the programs, which included three language programs: Spanish, Korean, and Vietnamese.

After five years of teaching without missing a day, I was asked to take a Bilingual Program Coordinator position for the school. Several candidates applied for the coordinator position, so I was shocked when the principal offered it to me. This position would be new for me because I had no experience outside of the classroom, so I was reluctant at first to accept it. But the principal said he had three reasons for recommending me for the position: "You are intelligent, hard-working, and resourceful. You also have experience teaching in a bilingual classroom." He said he would be the backbone that supported me. I felt encouraged to know the principal knew about my hard work and appreciated it.

Taking on a brand new position as the leader of a brand new program was a big risk. I felt it would be an enormous challenge and a big responsibility, but the position offered more freedom and a chance to work beyond the classroom, which I was yearning to do, so I accepted the offer.

The job was just as challenging as I had expected. I had to learn and teach the new programs to the other teachers, who didn't like to change or didn't agree with the bilingual program; they complained about the extra work, the program, and everything involved. Whenever they came to my office to complain, I took it personally and developed an ulcer from the stress. Yet I was persistent. I worked hard and diligently for long hours to help make the program successful.

As the bilingual population was rapidly growing in California, there was a need for trained bilingual teachers. The State Education Department was requiring the credential or certificate of competency of being a bilingual teacher. Then California State University of Los Angeles received a grant from the Federal Government to offer a Bilingual

Moving Mountains to Make It Happen

Teacher Training Program in Spanish, Korean, and Chinese. While I was working as a Bilingual Program Coordinator at Hobart Blvd. Elementary School, I was chosen as an Adjunct Professor of Education at California State University, Los Angeles to teach courses for Korean bilingual teacher candidates earning the bilingual emergency credential and to coordinate and organize a Korean Bilingual Teacher Training Program.

I enjoyed teaching the adult students in the college classes since they appreciated it and paid attention with full focus. The students used to say my voice was so soothing and pleasant that they could release all their stress in my class. The students suggested that I should work on the news broadcasts as an anchorwoman instead of at school. That was their ideal scene for me. In fact, that was my ideal job in my early twenties. But God had another plan.

In addition, I was consulting for developing the Korean Language and Culture Test for the Bilingual Competency Certificate for the state requirement. Also, I was called to administer the Korean Language Fluency Exam for the bilingual teacher candidates at the Los Angeles School District Office. I was wearing many hats, working for the school, the district, the Saturday Korean language and culture school, and the university Bilingual Teacher Training Program.

After two-and-a-half years of hard work as a Bilingual Program Coordinator at the school, I was promoted to an Instructional Advisor for the Region 5 office of the school district. I worked with several schools, communicating with the principals to help bilingual teachers, students, and parents. Later, I was promoted to Assistant Principal of Hoover Street Elementary School, which I believe at the time was the largest elementary school in the nation. The school had 2,700 students and 220 staff members on a year-round program with three tracks and three assistant principals. My track alone had 1,250 students with special education classes. There was no dull moment, especially with special ed. kids.

In the 1980s, the Ministry of Education in Korea was very interested in Korean bilingual education overseas and initiated the Bilingual Staff Development Project for American and Korean Educators. Educators who were working with the large population of Korean students were invited to participate. As the President of the Korean American Teachers Association, I led forty-five teachers from across the U.S. to Korea twice.

We traveled from Seoul to Kyung Joo, the ancient capital city, and visited many cultural sites, including Duk Soo Gung, Chang Kung Won, which were the palaces where the royal families lived, and a folk village near Seoul, which had an exhibition of ancient Korean houses, clothing, food, etc. We also attended performances of traditional Korean music and dance and many lectures about Korean language and culture. We enjoyed visiting schools where we could see how children were learning and interacting in the classrooms. All of us also enjoyed shopping at the open market at the South or East Gate in Seoul where we found great pieces of beautiful clothing, leather purses, and gift items at bargain prices. All of us appreciated the fast developing country with great buses and roads, and most of all, the government's utmost interest and its generosity in overseas education for the second generation Korean-Americans.

Besides returning to Korea to see my family and friends, this opportunity was very exciting for me because I got to meet educators from many different parts of the United States. Among them was a Superintendent from Tacoma, Washington. His district had many Korean students, and he invited me to take a principal position or work in the district office there. This offer was very tempting, but I didn't want to leave my friends and colleagues at school, or the beautiful weather of Southern California, or the lovely ocean view in Santa Monica, which had become my second home after Seoul, Korea. Now thinking back to that decision, I find that I was following my passion instead of seeking after a higher position that would bring an impression of worldly success. At that time, I was going where my heart led me.

DARING TO CHANGE

Despite not being a native English speaker, my persistence and my willingness to work hard, take responsibility, and have the initiative to start new projects afforded me the opportunity to make many contributions. The culmination of this hard work was when in 1984, I received a Korean Presidential Award for an outstanding contribution in the field of overseas education. It had taken me ten years to get there, but my dedication and tenacity had paid off.

We all have projects that seem too big, too difficult, or too impossible, but in the long run, perseverance with clear intention will always pay off, no matter what obstacles you face or how lofty your vision may be.

Under any circumstances, the power of a clear vision, perseverance, and meaningful coincidence will make even your seemingly impossible dreams a reality. Nor am I the only example of perseverance's benefits. Here are some other stories of perseverance, beginning with my parents' story of daring to change.

BEGINNING A NEW LIFE: MY PARENTS IN AMERICA

My parents came to the United States on November 3, 1985 after I became a citizen. In 2000, my mother was eligible to apply for U.S. citizenship. In order to make that happen, she needed to pass the citizenship test in English. Since she was educated during the Japanese occupancy of Korea, ev-

Moving Mountains to Make It Happen

erything in school was taught in Japanese. Now she was sixty years old and to apply for citizenship in the United States, she had to learn English, beginning with the alphabet.

She found a lady, Mrs. Lee, who was translating Korean and Japanese into English for many old people in that apartment complex, and they became friends. My mother had started to learn the alphabet from Mrs. Lee a year earlier. She also started learning American history. Then she collected sample questions and answers for the citizenship test from people who had already taken it and told her what kinds of questions they remembered were on it. She read over all these questions to memorize them.

Then for a month, my mother decided to stay with my youngest sister, who lived in Northern California at that time. My sister volunteered every day to teach her about American government and history. She memorized all of the important information as well as learning how to read those questions and answers in English. She made time to practice her English consistently every day. As a result, my mother passed the citizenship test in English. Later when my youngest sister had to take the test for citizenship, she passed her exam with flying colors because she had studied with my mother when she was teaching her. It reminds me of the old saying—life is full of give and take.

My mother's persistent efforts paid off and she became a proud U.S. citizen on February 22, 2000. Later, as a citizen, my mother could petition for her two younger daughters to get their green cards, and I was a sponsor. I have always been so proud of her tenacity to accomplish her goals. Later, my father also passed the test in Korean for U.S. citizenship in 2002. Both of my parents became proud U.S. citizens and both of them participated in voting as proud citizens.

Now that my parents were in the United States, they were both so proud of me as their young daughter who had not only come to the United States by herself, but also was able to support herself to become an independent and respected woman as a successful educator. They were especially proud that as a result of my many contributions to the community, I had become a Recipient of the Overseas Educator of the Year Award from the President of Korea in 1984. My parents were always grateful and proud of me that they were able to come to the United States, which was beyond their imagination, as a result of my efforts.

My father was sixty-four years old when he came to the U.S., but he decided to be involved in the community and to contribute to it. He volunteered his accounting skills for the "Korean Senior Citizens' Mutual Club," which grew to over 1,500 members, and later, he became the vice president and then the president of the organization. He received several awards from the Korean Consulate office, the Los Angeles

City Hall, and the Los Angeles County Office for his contributions to the seniors in the community.

My parents both made me proud and showed me once again that it is never too late to change and begin a new life, despite whatever obstacles are placed before you.

Perseverance through Visualization: Marilyn King

Marilyn King was an American Pentathlete who competed at the 1972 Olympics but injured her ankle and gave a deeply discouraging performance. But she didn't quit; instead, she kept training and qualified to attend the 1976 Olympics where she was thrilled to place thirteenth. Then she began preparing for the 1980 Olympics in Moscow. However, she was in a car accident and injured her back, which put her in bed for four months. She couldn't keep training physically, but Marilyn was absolutely focused on being ready and prepared for the Olympics, despite her back injury.

Marilyn spent her bedridden time watching films of world champion pentathletes, visualizing and feeling herself going through her event. She was using the images and feelings of excellence as her form of training. Although she had no opportunity to have proper physical training, she had managed to walk the course, visualizing herself performing optimally. This effort led to great results when she placed second at the trials for the Olympic Games in Moscow. Recent research has confirmed what Marilyn learned during that time—mental rehearsal and visualization can cause physical changes to the brain that will help the person to succeed.

Later, Marilyn became a motivational speaker, promoting what she calls "Olympic Thinking." She has come to realize that while mental rehearsal and visualization are powerful, they do not bring about exceptional achievements by themselves, but they must be aligned with vision, passion, and action. Today, Marilyn has gone on to promote her Olympic Thinking model to businesses and educational and peace organizations.

MOVING THE MOUNTAIN OF DISCRIMINATION: PAULL SHIN

Earlier, I told how Paul Shinn was adopted by an American soldier after the Korean War. Grateful for the gifts he had received and wanting to give back to his adopted country, Paull Shin eventually decided that he would serve his country through politics. But despite his good intentions, not everyone was excited by Paull's efforts.

Paull experienced a lot of racial discrimination just in his efforts to repay the country that had adopted him. When he decided to run for the Washington State House of Representatives in 1992, he went door to door to talk to people and try to receive their votes. In his autobiography, *An Exodus for Hope: The Footsteps of a Dream*, he tells about

Moving Mountains to Make It Happen

the reactions he received from some of the people he talked to. One man told him we already have too many Asian immigrants in the United States and that he should leave the country. Paull, who had already called the United States home for over thirty years, told him that the United States was made up of immigrants and that the man's own ancestors had been immigrants to this country, so if he were willing to leave the country, Paull would follow him.

Paull broke down barriers and discrimination by his honest nature and eagerness to serve others. For nine long months, he walked an average of eleven hours a day, and he visited 29,000 homes, wearing out four pairs of shoes. He also stood next to highways and busy intersections, waving signs to raise awareness of his candidacy. As he trudged from house to house for votes, he was struck by the irony of begging for votes in America when he had long ago begged for food in Korea and promised himself never again to allow himself to be a beggar.

Paull went on to have a successful career as a politician. He was the first Korean-American ever elected to the Washington State Legislature and went on to have a career of over twenty years in politics. Paull Shin is a living example of how mountains can be moved when you are passionate, you persevere, and you are willing to take action to help yourself and others.

Dare Questions

What would you say has been your greatest success in life?

_____
_____
_____

Did it come to you easily or did it take perseverance?

_____
_____
_____

What qualities or tools of perseverance did you use to succeed and bring about that accomplishment?

_____
_____
_____
_____

How might you use those same qualities or tools to succeed in your current vision for what you want your life to be?

_____
_____
_____
_____

CHAPTER 9

Never Giving Up

"Never give in. Never give in. Never, never, never, never—in nothing, great or small, large or petty—never give in, except to convictions of honor and good sense."
— Winston Churchill

Whenever you want to succeed at something, there will be obstacles in your way. Some will be small, but some will feel as big as boulders, and the bigger the goal you have, the bigger the obstacles. But that doesn't mean that a big obstacle needs to stop you. It may take more work. It might take longer to accomplish. But it can be done.

Albert Einstein understood this. Today, Einstein is universally acknowledged as a genius, perhaps the smartest man who ever lived, but he knew better than to believe he was born a genius. What did he attribute his success to? He said, "It's not that I'm so smart; it's just that I stay with problems longer."

The truth is that anything can be accomplished if you stick with it, work at it regularly, and when obstacles get in the way, rather than giving up, you find a way to work around, through, under, or over them. So many people never achieve their dreams or make the changes they want to see in their lives because they do give up. Don't be one of them. Don't be afraid of hard work, and don't be afraid of failure. As football coach Vince Lombardi said, "It's not whether you get knocked down. It's whether you get up again."

To illustrate this point, I have another story of my experiences during the Korean War to tell you.

A Mother's Determination

This is another miraculous story that took place during the Korean War in the winter of 1951. At that time, the communists again advanced into the South, recapturing Seoul, the South Korean Capital.

As a child, I fled with my mother, sister, and baby brother from Seoul. We first went to Anyang where we stayed until the North Korean Army and Chinese communists reached the city. Then we had to flee to Suwon, about twenty-one miles south of Seoul. At night, bombs were dropped around the city. They were so bright and the noise was so powerful that it opened up the rice paper door and we screamed with fear while Mother held us together to protect us.

Since the communist soldiers would be in Suwon for some time, my mother decided that we would go to the city of Inchon where the Korean military police were located, so we would be more secure. It was a cold winter and it had snowed. Everything was frozen and the path we walked was slippery. My mother dressed me in a red coat with a cotton lining and I had a hat to cover my ears. My sister had a wool red coat and also a hat. I was carrying a bag of diapers for my baby brother on my back.

We started out early in the morning to follow the hundreds of people through the narrow walkway in the rice fields. Everything was covered with snow and ice. We couldn't stop to eat even if we had something to eat because there were people following close behind us and there was nowhere to eat in the snow.

As we were walking in the crowd, I heard a baby crying. I was looking at the snow covered farm field at a distance where I saw a mother lying in the field on a blanket. She had just given birth, I believe, and the baby was alive and crying in the freezing winter cold on the icy field with no one to carry him or his mother to safety. For the first time in my life, I felt deeply sad and understood how tragic life can be.

We were so exhausted from not eating or drinking all day, and my shoulder was hurting by carrying a diaper bag for my baby brother. My mother was carrying a bundle with some valuable belongings on her head, as well as carrying my baby brother on her back. My sister started crying out of hunger and exhaustion, and slowed down the line. Everyone was hurrying to get to Inchon City so my sister was pushed aside and she fell off the path, landing near the stream below. I began crying and calling out for my mom, and I ran down the hill to bring her back to the line. Now, we couldn't see my mother.

Meanwhile, my mother was approached by a young woman who offered to help her by carrying her bundle on her head. My mother thanked her and gave her the bundle, but after a few minutes, my mother lost sight of her. The young woman had run away with my mother's belongings. My mother had to chase her because the bundle contained everything she had, including expensive clothes and items we could use to buy food. My sister and I soon lost my mother since she was chasing after the woman, and there were hundreds and hundreds of refugees in this exodus, so all we could do was keep walking in the right direction toward Inchon City.

Eventually, the long, narrow path through the farmland ended, and by the time we got to the large plaza, it was dark out. There were hundreds of people standing around, and I didn't know how to find my mother. I was holding my sister's hand and we both were crying and calling out in the crowd for my mother in the plaza where the police station was.

Meanwhile, my mother was shocked that she had also lost us. She was shocked with the reality, but she never gave up on finding us. For hours, she asked everyone she saw whether they had seen her daughters. Finally, my mother met a woman who said, "I saw two pretty girls wearing red coats and standing at the plaza near the police office. They were crying and calling out, "Mom!" My mother went running to find us with the baby on her back in the cold winter night.

I don't remember how long my sister and I stood there, crying in the cold, dark, and scary winter night. Eventually, a military policeman heard about us and took us inside the office and planned to report us as being lost children. I remember how warm that place was. I felt my frozen body was melting down. The officer offered us a bowl of soup with barley rice. We ate it in a few minutes since we hadn't eaten all day. There was a straw mat in the office so we sat on it and waited for my mom and fell asleep. Next thing I knew, I heard my mother's voice. It was the next morning and she was waking us up. We were soon all crying with joy. What a miraculous moment it was!

My mother thanked the officers and then we continued our journey to find a place to live in the city. When I think back to that time, I realize what a smart young woman my mother was to have us wear red coats so we would stand out better in the crowd. I thank God that we were saved from being orphans in the war and that my mother never gave up until she found us on that cold icy winter night.

Never giving up is absolutely necessary if you want to achieve your goals. Let's look at Helen Keller's story as another example.

Don't Give Up on Yourself or Others: Anne Sullivan and Helen Keller

Helen Keller is one of the best known people in American history for overcoming adversity. Not only did she achieve her remarkable goals, but she made significant contributions to society.

Helen was born in Alabama in 1880. When Helen was nineteen months old, she became very ill with "brain fever." Today, it is believed she actually suffered from scarlet fever. The disease completely destroyed her ability to see or to hear.

Her parents took her to Boston, Massachusetts to attend the Perkins Institute for the Blind. There she met a tutor, Anne Sullivan, who taught Helen to read Braille, to write, and to communicate effectively despite her blindness and being deaf.

Helen became determined not to let her handicaps hold her back from experiencing a normal life. In fact, she went on to college—something unusual for women at the time—attending Radcliffe with Anne Sullivan's help. She mastered several languages and graduated with honors. She then became a writer of articles for books, newspapers, and magazines. In 1903, her book, *The Story of My Life*, was published and it would be translated into more than fifty languages.

Before the end of her life in 1968, Helen received numerous honorary degrees and awards for her humanitarian work and the inspiration she provided for the blind and the deaf, including the prestigious Presidential Medal of Freedom.

Helen Keller never gave up on what she wanted to accomplish because she realized Anne Sullivan never gave up on her. Can you imagine what her life would have been like if Anne Sullivan had given up on Helen or if Helen had given up on herself? Because of Helen and Anne's efforts, millions of deaf and blind children and their parents have been inspired to believe they could live happy and successful lives and contribute to society. Because these two women never gave up, the world is a better place today.

DARING TO CHANGE

Helen Keller once stated that we need to see how the troubles we experience actually benefit us. She was quoted as saying, "The struggle of life is one of our greatest blessings. It makes us patient, sensitive, and Godlike. It teaches us that although the world is full of suffering, it is also full of the overcoming of it."

If Helen Keller could succeed despite all the obstacles she faced, think of what you can do if you just stay persistent.

DARE QUESTIONS

Have you ever given up when faced by a challenge in your life? Do you regret it now?

_____
_____
_____
_____
_____

When have you been tempted to give up but you didn't? Do you feel you made the right decision in staying the course?

_____
_____
_____
_____
_____

What are you tempted to give up on now? Envision what the future will be like if you do give up. Then envision what it will be like if you don't give up.

_____
_____
_____
_____
_____

PART FOUR

Transforming Your Life for the Next Chapter

CHAPTER 10

Living Your Passion and Finding Your Purpose

"Thoughts lead on to purposes; purposes go forth in action; actions form habits; habits decide character; and character fixes our destiny."
— Tryon Edwards

Are you still asking yourself, "What is my life purpose?" Many of us don't have a clue what our purpose should be. Or maybe you know you have a purpose, but you're not sure what it is. Most people live life without ever finding their true life purpose. Your purpose is not just your job or to make money, but to find a larger vision—to find what is meaningful to you in your life; what you are passionate about—and then to use that passion to find a purpose in life and make a difference in the world.

DARING TO CHANGE

To find your passion and purpose, you need to feel connected to your soul and your inner wisdom. In her book *Happy for No Reason*, Marci Shimoff states, "When you are clear about your passions, you're lit by a fire inside that shows you what to do in each moment. You are led to inspired action. You know *what* you want to do in life, but you may not know *how* it will happen. Inspiration will lead you to the *how*."

But will your inspired action work? It will if you love learning and are energized by the journey toward being masterful in your own life, and if you are focused on being the best you can be for yourself, your loved ones, and the world. If you're action-oriented and love achieving what you set out to do, you can do anything you put your mind to.

There are people who will try to talk you out of your new vision, such as your parents or best friend. They will console your soul by saying, "How can you leave a respectful and secure job for life?" Don't listen to them. Follow your passion and purpose, and if necessary, keep it to yourself, or only share it with like-minded people who will support you in it. *Living your True Purpose* will remove all your excuses for why you are not doing what you were born to do. Finding your life purpose can help you to be happier and livelier than ever before. When you follow your calling or purpose, you can experience a more fulfilling and passionate life. Your life will never be the same again.

Living Your Passion and Finding Your Purpose

In his book *Reinvention: How to Make the Rest of Your Life the Best of Your Life*, Brian Tracy reveals how every one of us is engineered for success, and with the right focus, we can reinvent ourselves and put an end to the chronic stress, unhappiness, and dissatisfaction we might feel in our careers and lives.

Reinventing yourself means daring to change. Nothing says we have to stay stuck in a rut in our lives. Nothing says even that we can't have a wonderful career and then reinvent ourselves to have a wonderful second or third career. Perhaps your purpose in life might even change, or what you thought was your purpose is only the beginning to an even bigger purpose you haven't yet had the vision for. With passion, you can reinvent yourself and discover that new or greater purpose.

With passion, you can realize that life is an adventure. When you have an adventure, you are free to explore your true nature and all it has to offer you. Of course, you never know if what you want to explore will be discovered, but you don't know if you don't try, and if you take action toward creating the life you want to live, your life is bound to become better. And don't forget that life is not solely about the arrival, but also the journey. Following your passion is about the process of creating the life you want to live and living your life passionately. Living a passionate life each day is itself the fulfill-

DARING TO CHANGE

ment of following your passion. And if your passion changes, don't hesitate to reinvent yourself and live a new passion.

After teaching first grade for about five years, I began to feel the need to reinvent myself. Although I loved teaching young children, I was restless because I was repeating the same thing, the same routine, and seeing the same people, working in the same building day after day. You know your physical environment affects your life. I was feeling stuck and ready for a new challenge. I was yearning for more fulfillment, more meaning, more passion and freedom, and to have all parts of my life in alignment with who I wanted to be. I was motivated to transform my life, and I was committed to making changes that would bring me new activities, new people, new places, and peace, freedom, and sustainable excitement.

I was dreaming about a new adventure like owning a business so I could be in charge of my own time, with my own ideas, doing creative work, and meeting new people—I wanted more freedom. I yearned to discover what was out there beyond my classroom walls. I became restless and wanted to find out what I truly wanted to do with the rest of my life.

When I learned that the UCLA extension office was offering a career counseling and aptitude test, I went to take it. The test would determine which careers I had the greatest aptitude for, and my highest score turned out to be as an entrepreneur. I was so surprised to see that the score matched exactly what I was feeling. But I was scared to leave the security of my job, and I wasn't clear what to do to make a career transition. I didn't make any change at that time, but I held onto my desire for more freedom and kept the idea of entrepreneurship always in the back of my mind.

When I was promoted to Assistant Principal of a school with 2,700 students, the school was on a year-round schedule, which only allowed me twenty days vacation out of the whole year. As a school administrator, I worked long hours. I started my work at 7:30 a.m., and most days I stayed late waiting for parents to pick up their children from after school programs. There was never a dull moment with that many students, parents, and with so many staff members. But I missed the luxury of having a long summer vacation like other teachers.

A lot of people might consider me a "Jill of All Trades" because I do a number of things at once. It never surprised me to walk into my office to find troubled kids waiting, parents showing up, phones ringing, meetings to prepare, and a visitor who wanted to see me. And while I stayed on top of it all, I began to feel disconnected from my own life. My salary was higher than the salaries of most principals at small schools because my school had the largest student enrollment with a Title I program on a year-round schedule. But I felt like I was running around in circles without having much passion any longer for my work. I was remembering my aptitude test at UCLA career center, years ago, for being an entrepreneur. I was yearning for something that would make me feel more passionate, and I was thinking about my life purpose again. I had twenty vacation days, but even that had to be divided into two vacations of ten days each since there was no one to substitute for me when I took my vacation. I felt I was burned out on the job.

One day, I finally realized why I felt stuck in a "nine to five" job, so to speak. I was at the same place with the same routine, same people, and same work. I started to ask myself, "Where did my passion go?" I was looking for something freer, and more creative and meaningful, more exciting and different, and I was wondering, "Is this all there is in life?" I now felt exhausted much of the time. I felt like I was losing my zest.

We've all been there. We've all had a crisis in our lives when we know we need to change, but we don't know how. You probably are feeling that right now. It's probably why you decided to read this book. I can tell you that you'll get through it, but when you get to that point where you start to feel you are losing your zest, you need to make a choice: You can continue working with less joy, or you can make a change to living a life that is true to your own personality, character, or spirit. You then become a more conscious person.

Living Your Passion and Finding Your Purpose

If living your dream from childhood is not enough, search your soul for a new passion. Then pursue that passion with all your heart and don't let anyone's ignorance and negative attitude stop you. This is the time when you need to pull on your greatest resource—your faith—to be your guide.

Mary Morrissey, author of *Building Your Dreams*, believes the yearning in us is a call from God to change and follow our dreams:

> In your life at this moment, there is something in you that is yearning for a greater expression. If you are not in touch with that yearning, you are not in touch with your true self. If you lack desire, you have stopped listening to God....True desire, not just self-centered interest, comes from God.

When your soul is yearning for something, you have to trust it and trust God. Remember, we are co-creators with God and the universe. When we do our part, they will step in and help us along the way to make the changes we need, even if we aren't yet clear on what those changes are.

So, finally, I started to examine my own life's inner yearnings. I had been in the education field for over twenty-five years at the time, and I had begun to feel my passion leaving me for the last several years. But for whatever reason, through promotions and perhaps fear of leaving a secure job with a good income, and maybe fear of disappointing my parents, I did not make a change. I hesitated to leave my comfort zone. I wondered when or if I would.

When is the time to change? When will we change and go after an area of our lives that is stuck or has been lying dormant for months or years? When will we stop focusing on the repetitive life we are living when it isn't bringing us the joy, passion, love, and fulfillment we desire?

Personal success expert Brian Tracy attests, "It's not until you deal with the dissatisfactions of the present that you can move onward and upward to create the wonderful future that is possible for you. And it is possible."

For me, making a change began with acknowledging rather than suppressing how I felt, and then asking myself, "How do I want to feel?" I was thinking that any career that calls for flexibility and quick change, and that didn't involve any kind of routine or set schedule, but more freedom and work of a creative nature, would suit my adventurous, energetic, and enthusiastic nature. Freedom is a word I can relate to. I felt I needed to change the status quo and relieve my chronic stress. Whatever career I would choose, I still would be an educator, and I would enjoy working with the public, so I wanted some element of teaching included in it, but in a larger setting than a public school. I remembered my career

Living Your Passion and Finding Your Purpose

aptitude test result from many years ago at UCLA had been for Entrepreneurship.

I love learning new things, so since the 1980s, I had been taking seminars on the weekends and attending transformational talks, seminars, and conferences such as by Werner Erhard, the founder of EST, which later became Landmark Education, and listening to America's top self-growth speakers like Anthony Robbins and Jack Canfield, as well as attending spiritual seminars that promoted greater emotional and spiritual wellbeing.

As my yearning continued, one day I unexpectedly received a flyer describing an "Empowerment" workshop in New York described as "The Art of Creating Your Life As You Want It." It was the perfect title for me, and it couldn't be better. I have no idea how that flyer came to me since I had never received any seminar flyer before. I used to simply look up seminars I wanted to attend. Receiving it at this time felt like an opportune coincidence, and it felt like I was at a turning point. As I read the flyer, I felt more and more that this workshop was for me. God had heard my desires and felt my restlessness and yearnings. I was so excited. I flew to New York and took a train along the Hudson River to attend the workshop during winter break. That experience was the culmination of everything I had been learning from all the seminars and workshops I'd attended in the past. Plus, it showed me how to start to create the life I wanted NOW.

At the workshop, I first learned, "When you have a compelling vision, you can let go of your self-limiting beliefs easier and create what you want." That's exactly what I did with my life coming to the U.S. from Korea. "In order to create new, visualize your vision in your mind on a daily basis and affirm your vision daily out loud." It was a powerful message that awakened me!

The leaders, Gail Straub and David Gershon, the authors of the bestselling book *Empowerment: The Art of Creating Your Life As You Want It*, were truly passionate about empowering every person to create the life he/she wanted. Their language and content were so different from what I usually heard in an educational setting. They were inspiring and uplifting everyone with love and profound expertise, and they were traveling the world making money by inspiring people to live their visions. I felt that was my passion. That was what I wanted to do. I felt so empowered that I wanted to share this message with my community. I had found a new passion to empower others to find their own passion and to create the lives they wanted.

As an educator, I was always interested in learning new things that would help me teach better. Now I became fascinated with self-growth teachings. I was finding answers to why I held certain inner feelings and beliefs, and why I took action the way I did. Through the self-growth seminars and workshops I began to attend, I could understand better about my father and mother, their interactions with each other, our family's dynamics, and how all of that had influenced me into becoming the person I am now. I started a self-improvement plan, developing and learning new ways of thinking through self-growth seminars and workshops. And I felt so fortunate that I could learn anything I wanted in this country of America.

My father and mother had never experienced such learning opportunities; they had only been able to learn from their parents and society. By attending these seminars, I came to understand and forgive my father; I forgave him for his lack of communication and interaction with us growing up, and for his disrespectful and domineering behaviors to my mother.

From that time on, I have felt that I am here to explore everything, and each day I wake up loving my freedom and looking forward to new opportunities for creativity. I discovered that transformation is possible if we practice new lessons and the art of conscious living.

As an educator, I knew that God had given me the opportunity to motivate and influence young souls for more than twenty-five years. Now He had given me a new purpose and new ideas for how to empower and inspire people at large through my teaching experience. I *am* a teacher for life. Now I would find a new way to teach the grown-ups.

I started contemplating a career transition as someone who leads empowerment workshops. But as I contemplated the transition, the fear came. I began to ask myself:

- When I leave my current job, where I have spent my entire career, will I lose my identity, security, and status?
- Is it the right time and right thing to do?
- Will my new career be successful?
- How will my parents, friends, and coworkers feel about it?

I remembered some wise words I had once heard from Dr. Daniel Amen, the author of the book, *Change Your Brain, Change Your Life*: "When you are eighteen, you worry about what everybody is thinking of you; when you are forty, you don't give a darn what anybody thinks of you; when you are sixty, you realize nobody's been thinking about you at all." When I heard that, I laughed and laughed. I felt it gave me the permission to move forward, and it was very true. Most of the time, people are too busy worrying about their own lives to worry about you. It is much better to spend your time thinking about and doing the things that will achieve your

Living Your Passion and Finding Your Purpose

goals rather than worrying what others will think. So I decided I wouldn't discuss my career transition with anybody, not even with my mother. Then I started to think:

- I am willing to see my truth instead of tolerating something that is going nowhere.
- It is my life. What is my true purpose in the next chapter of my life?

I was repeating these thoughts over and over, yet I still stayed at my job.

I was surprised to see myself taking so much time to make a career transition due to my fears. I realized part of my fear was because I had much more to lose than when I had first come to the United States with only one bag. Now I was afraid of losing what I had. To overcome this fear, I started getting rid of a lot of accumulated stuff I didn't need, and I told myself, "The simple life is a great life," and "The more possessions you have, the less freedom you have." In the meantime, I was asking God to guide me to the right path. I had been working ever since I was a sophomore in college, so now was the time to follow my new inspired passion to be an empowerment seminar leader and a speaker who would empower others to live the empowered lives they wanted with passion.

Then the last day of June, right before the new school year began on July 1 for the year-round school, it was announced that three out of four administrators, including the principal, were to be transferred to other schools. I was one of them. I was so surprised about this bombshell announcement with very short notice. Then the next day, the school district's Region Superintendent called to tell me that he wanted me to be a principal after this transfer to another school with an excellent principal, because, with my experience, I would also be an excellent principal. I was at a turning point—either stay to be a principal, or become free to live the dream of being an Empowerment speaker and seminar leader and expressing who I am in the world with freedom and passion. Here was another synchronicity that happened for me to make the transition easier so I could follow my heart's desire.

You know things happen for a reason, and you know the people and experiences you attract into your life—good and not so good—are here to teach you something. *This transfer was a synchronistic event given to me to follow my new passionate dream.* The author Deepak Chopra said in one of his talks, "Synchronicity is an anonymous gift from God given in a state of grace." Yes! I had received His grace when He opened a new door for me to make my transition easier for a new purpose in life.

I now trusted that God had something better in store for me. I was no longer interested in becoming a principal; instead, I was ready to use the power of intentional creation and my freedom to attract more of what I wanted into my life.

Living Your Passion and Finding Your Purpose

My new passion gave me a chance to transform myself and move into a new chapter in life. My vision was to become an inspirational speaker and a writer, so I could share my experiences to empower others to create the lives they wanted with passion. I soon began my new career. I was so excited to offer empowerment workshops to the public in my community and to business organizations. Because of my courage and passion, I became the first woman in the community to initiate empowerment workshops.

I was invited to be a keynote speaker at the universities and conferences in Seoul, Korea. It was an exciting experience to talk to so many enthusiastic young university students and adults to answer their questions about how they could empower themselves.

And now I am writing this book and being a radio columnist in Southern California, something I never dreamed I would do. I spend significant time every day working to improve myself and my life, using my creativity and participating in creating a better world for people everywhere. Life has become an exciting adventure again!

I feel I am an awakening woman. Each day I wake up loving my freedom and looking forward to new and creative opportunities for expressing myself. To me, happiness is doing what you love, pursuing your passion, helping other people by sharing courageous experiences to empower their lives, and achieving emotional and financial peace of mind. If you can use your cheer, warmth, good humor, and love for life to inspire others to do the same and make this world a happier place, you will fulfill your purpose and have an amazing life as well.

Now, you may be thinking, "That's all well for you, Helen. You found your passion, but how do I find mine?"

Here is some help to get you started on your quest to find your passion:

To find your passion, according to Janet and Chris Attwood, coauthors of the book, *The Passion Test,* you should make a list of the ten most important things you can think of that would give you a life of joy, passion, and fulfillment. Begin each with a verb relating to being, doing, or having, which completes the sentence.

When my life is ideal, I am _____.

For example:

Being

- When my life is ideal, I am a bestselling author and successful inspiring speaker uplifting people internationally.

- When my life is ideal, I am flowing with life easily and effortlessly.

Living Your Passion and Finding Your Purpose

Having

- When my life is ideal, I am owning a beautiful house overlooking the ocean and enjoy living in it.
- When my life is ideal, I am enjoying perfect health and a radiant body.

Doing

- When my life is ideal, I am traveling the world first class with my friends and loved ones.
- When my life is ideal, I am helping people live their highest visions internationally.

Picture your ideal life. What are you doing? Who are you with? Where are you? How do you feel?

Once you have determined your ten passions, then compare and prioritize them until you narrow them down to your top five passions, and then you may narrow them down further. It's recommended that you do this process every six months to keep your passions current and alive.

Also, Deepak Chopra, in an article titled "Discover Your Life's True Purpose," offers a list of clues to determine both whether you are and aren't living your purpose. A few of his points that really resonate with me are:

- You lose track of time. Instead of watching the clock or thinking about what you'd rather be doing, you're fully immersed in present moment awareness.

- You're excited about the unfolding possibilities and the opportunity to serve others as you express your unique gifts and talents.

- You don't seek approval, security, or control. Knowing that your true source of abundance and creativity is infinite, you don't get caught up in the ego's archetypical power struggles.

In other words, when you find your life's purpose, you feel good about what you are doing. You wake up excited about what you have to do that day. If you wake up dreading the day, you're on the wrong path so it's time to try something new—it's time to dare to change.

Your life will always express what is going on deep inside you. Therefore, if your results are out of line with your stated intentions, it's time to do some self-examination. Keep at it. Your passion is in your heart and you will find it. Have faith that once you set the intention, and then follow up with action with all your heart, God will co-create with you to make it happen.

Here is a quote by T. Menlo which I believe best illustrates the concept of developing a higher purpose:

"If each day of your life represents a sparkle of light, at your life's end, you will have illuminated the world."

Let me tell you the story of someone who woke up every day believing in his dream, making it his life purpose, and in the end, that dream did illuminate the world.

COLONEL SANDERS: TURNING YOUR DREAM INTO YOUR LIFE PURPOSE

At age sixty-six, Colonel Sanders decided he wanted to go into the chicken business. He believed he had the absolutely best chicken recipe in the world and he wanted to share it with everyone.

First, he tried going to restaurants in his community and offering the owners his recipe in exchange for a percentage of the profits from the fried chicken sales. When people in his own town turned him down, he remained so convinced that he had a winning recipe that he decided to try elsewhere. Soon he was traveling from town to town in his old automobile, trying to sell his recipe to restaurants all over the United States. And over and over, at every place he visited, he was told, "No." Eventually, he had so little money that he had to sleep in his car, but he didn't let that stop him. Colonel Sanders loved his fried chicken recipe so much that he kept trying to sell it.

Because Colonel Sanders believed that success could always lie with the next person he spoke to, he never gave up. After being rejected 2,000 times over the course of two years, Colonel Sanders' dedication and hard work finally paid off. He found someone to buy his recipe, and soon after, his fried chicken became so immensely popular that today, 18,000 Kentucky Fried Chicken restaurants can be found in 120 countries all across the world.

Colonel Sanders became a multi-millionaire and lived to be ninety-six years old. He would live to see how successful his fried chicken recipe had become. He had turned fried chicken into his life purpose—but it was also a purpose that included making people happy when they gathered around the table to enjoy his special recipe. I'm sure Colonel Sanders went to bed at night feeling happy to know that millions of people were enjoying his fried chicken.

Happiness is doing what you love, pursuing your passions, helping other people along the way, living for a cause, and achieving financial and emotional peace of mind. As you become happier, I believe you will become unstoppable and live a life like you have never envisioned.

I believe that if you listen to your heart and then choose your own life purpose with your passion, you will be happy. The happiness comes from doing what you love to do.

DARE QUESTIONS

If you currently feel empty, describe any specific thoughts and feelings.

_____

_____

If there is a purpose in your life at this time, what do you think it might be?

_____

_____

_____

Are you inspired by what you do?

_____

_____

_____

What would you really like to do? What is your passion?

_____

_____

_____

_____

What do you love to do when you have free time?

_____

_____

DARING TO CHANGE

What would you like to contribute to the world?

_____
_____
_____

What fears are standing in your way and how might they be irrational?

_____
_____
_____

What is one thing you can do today to move beyond one or more of your fears and toward your passion?

_____
_____
_____

CHAPTER 11

Becoming Courageous

"Life is about moments.
Don't wait for them, create them."
— Tony Robbins

Life is constant change. A life without change has no growth and your life can become stagnant. Some people fear change, some people resist change, and some people welcome it. Change can take you out of your comfort zone. It's easier to keep things as they are, but life never stands still. Change happens when you are no longer interested in something, or there is no hope, or you want to follow a dream more aligned with your true nature.

When you have a compelling dream, the experience of change can help you to be transformed from the old you. You can make this change by facing your fears as I did with my new life in the New World. Finding the courage to be courageous and follow your compelling vision is the key to achieving your new life of purpose. Your life without courage can be nothing but a fantasy because courage is the fuel you need to take action. Find and use your courage to act on your goal and vision for your life.

If your dream is establishing a new career, empower yourself. Don't live in fear. Affirm and visualize your dream, believe it's possible, and think and say it positively. Your new choice is to go for it. Fear is only in your mind. When you feel worry, doubt, and dwell on how unfair life is, you become stuck and life becomes limited. This kind of victim feeling limits your vision of what life can be.

Don't be a victim. Be a hero. Be the hero of your own life. How do you become a hero? By being courageous. By doing your best. Doing your best and striving to be the best is how you show you are courageous. When you choose to create your own path, to do something that no one else has done before, you are being courageous. When people are afraid to do something or tell you that you can't do it, then they are victims of their own fears. But you are a hero if you do it anyway, and when you do it, then you make your dreams happen. True courage is having the determination to follow your passion and dreams, no matter what they are, and without caring about what others think. That is true courage and how you become the hero of your own life.

Adopt a life of courage. Courage is not the absence of fear, but taking action in the presence of it. Life coach Dr. Marilyn Gustin says about courage, "The essence of courage is about living wholeheartedly. Walk your path with faith, courage, passion, and determination. Keep your belief in yourself and walk into your new journey. Courage is not losing enthusiasm because of failure."

Take a step toward what you want, and once you change, it will be hard to go back to the way things were. Trust that the doors will open before you. Trust that God will co-create with you and guide you.

The stories we tell ourselves determine our lives. We either empower ourselves, or we dis-empower ourselves when we allow our story to defend us and dictate the course of our lives. The stories we choose to tell ourselves dictate who we are and what we're capable of becoming or not becoming. We need to revisit the past and bring awareness and closure to it so we can be released from ingrained insecurity, fears, and regret.

To ignite your confidence and reclaim your courage, you must step into the highest vision of who you are. To do so is another way of asking God to help you. Within each painful experience are seeds of wisdom and opportunities for new beginnings.

When fear arises, ask yourself where this fear comes from? Consider that if it is an irrational fear; it could be based in something from your childhood that made it relevant then, but it no longer is. For example, you felt fear of abandonment from a childhood trauma, such as being lost in the shopping mall and fearing your parents had left you behind. Now you are an adult and are able to deal with going to the mall and finding your way home, and you can also handle any other situations that come into your life.

Take time now to make a list of your fears and why you have them:

	I FEAR	**I HAVE THIS FEAR BECAUSE**
1.		
2.		
3.		
4.		
5.		

Now that you know what your fears are, and you can see how they are holding you back and may be irrational, you can begin to turn them around. Another great exercise to help yourself through this process is to ask yourself what you would do if you were not afraid. Spend some time filling in the sentences below (I did the first one as an example for you):

Example: If I were not afraid, I would leave my dead-end job and go back to school to get my degree so I can have a better life.

If I were not afraid, I would

_____

If I were not afraid, I would

_____

If I were not afraid, I would

_____

If I were not afraid, I would

_____

If I were not afraid, I would

_____

Perhaps in this process, you will discover, like I did, that you want to help others to get over the same kinds of obstacles that you have faced. You may have taken the pain and obstacles of your past and said, "I want to share my story and help others." Then pick up the pieces and move on to live an empowering life by empowering others. Whatever you choose to do, by doing it, you are empowering yourself and serving as an example of inspiration to others. We all have the ability to create a meaningful life for ourselves that empowers us and others.

Author Benjamin Disraeli said, "Man is not the creature of circumstances; circumstances are the creatures of men." When things become too tough for you, keep the faith and remember you are just a co-creator. The universe is working to help you realize your dreams. Have confidence in yourself. Stop hiding your power. Stand up with courage. Remember that you were born into this world with nothing, and everything you see around you, you created for yourself. The truth is that if you have done it before, you can do it again, no matter what!

I won't pretend that this process is easy. It takes courage to face what is not working in our lives. Fortunately, I have an energetic and enthusiastic nature. I have a natural and enthusiastic ability to adapt to almost any situation that comes along. I feel that almost any career, especially entrepreneurship that calls for flexibility and quick change—and that doesn't involve any kind of routine or set schedule—will suit me according to my career aptitude test and my desire.

I had all of these strong character traits to help me pursue my passion, yet I stayed in the same career for more than twenty years where I felt stifled and drained. You might be feeling the same way. But my fears were holding me back and whispering to me, "It isn't easy. You will fail. You don't know what you are doing. You are a fool...."

When I contemplated why I was afraid to make the change, I focused on security, income, status, and my identity. I was surprised to discover how important the security was for me.

I found my courage through rediscovering my own spirit of adventure from earlier in my life. I remembered that I had started with nothing and created everything around me. I told myself, "I've done it before, so I can do it again." Yet, every time I was feeling the urge to leave my job, I kept working harder and ignoring my inner voices of discontent. I was a good example of the saying, "The more you have, the harder it is to give it up." When you don't have anything, you have nothing to lose if you pick yourself up and create a new something. But when you have accumulated more, you don't want to lose it, so you can be stuck living in your comfort zone with pain and discontent.

Often we wonder how we distinguish our inner voice or the voice of God from less reliable chatter—my ego, my history, or my fear. Here is one of my favorite teaching stories about a man who received every possible signal that God was guiding him.

DARING TO CHANGE

IGNORING OUR INNER VOICE AND GOD

There was once a man who had a deep faith in God. He was always telling his friends that his chaotic life would work itself out because God would take care of him. One day, a huge storm caused serious flooding in the town where this man lived. While other members of the community packed their belongings and fled, the man stayed put, believing that God would take care of him. The water began to seep under his doors and through the windows. A fire truck drove by, and rescue workers yelled to the man, "Come on; you can't stay here!"

"No!" he said to them, "God will take care of me!" Soon the water was waist high, the streets turning to rivers. A Coast Guard boat came past the man's house. The crew yelled out to him, "Swim out and come on board!" "No!" the man yelled back, "God will take care of me."

The rain kept pouring down until the man's entire house was flooded. Then a helicopter flew over his house, and the pilot spotted the man praying on his roof. "You down there, grab hold of the ladder and we'll take you to safety!" Again the man proclaimed his conviction: "God will take care of me."

Finally, the man drowned. At the pearly gates of heaven, the man had never felt more betrayed. "My God," he said, "I put my faith in you and prayed to you for my rescue. You told me you would always take care of me, yet when I needed you most, you were not there." "What do you mean?" replied God. "I sent you a fire truck, a boat, and a helicopter. What more did you want?"

How many times do we ignore our inner voice? If the man had listened when he prayed, he would have understood how God was trying to help him. Our inner voice is ready to help us move toward our highest good anytime we choose to listen. We can communicate with our still and small voice every day, if we desire. When we pay attention, sit quietly, and listen to it, the voice amplifies.

Change happens when you are no longer interested in something, or there is no hope, or you want to follow a dream more aligned with your true nature and higher purpose. Whatever fears you face, if you open yourself to the possibilities of change and you decide to be brave in the face of fear, doors will open to help make that change possible for you.

Do you want to change your life? Make a decision for what you want in your life. Be bold once again. Be brave enough to take action. Test things out and be persistent. If you fail, get up again, and smile, and keep moving. This is the courage to change and help you truly live your life. What would my life have been like if I had not dared to change? I don't even want to imagine that. Neither do you want to live a life without making a change. Plant the seed and visualize the life you want and watch that life grow.

DARING TO CHANGE

DARE QUESTIONS

Ask yourself again: What would I do if I were not afraid?

_____
_____
_____

We often call brave people "heroes." Who are your heroes and why do you think these people are heroic?

_____
_____
_____

How can you live a life inspired by your heroes and the changes they made in their lives?

_____
_____
_____

What would it feel like if you were the hero of your own life? Take time to write about what life would be like if you were full of courage, despite any fears, and you trusted that everything would work out for the best.

_____
_____
_____

CHAPTER 12

Doing What You Love to Live the Life You Want

> "Change is the essence of life. Be willing to surrender what you are for what you could become."
> — Anonymous

It's often said that if you do what you love, you'll never work another day in your life. It was clear to me that being an inspirational speaker and writing this book was what I was meant to do. I began to fulfill my purpose and allow the passion within me to help others create the lives they wanted. Passion was the key; it's what life is all about. When we find our passion, our lives begin to change.

Are you living the life you want? Or is your life determined by others?

Sometimes the only way to create the life you want—and deserve—is to let go of the past and begin anew. That can be scary because sudden change leaves us without a known blueprint for our lives.

I know from my own experience how hard it can be to start over. As you know, I started my life over in a new land all by myself, with a broken heart, no funds, or the support of my family. In the end, this challenging experience turned out to be my greatest opportunity because it gave me a second life to create something new. It wasn't easy. I had to overcome fear, negativity, and self-blame in order to move ahead and manifest my dream to become an "independent and respected woman."

The good news is that we can recover from what is difficult. We can overcome absolutely everything. Each one of us has untapped potential and unmapped reservoirs of strength that we can draw from.

Now that you are at the end of this book, it's time for you to make a decision. Are you going to change? Are you going to embrace the wonderful possibilities that lie ahead for you in life? This moment is a new beginning for you. This is a day of new beginnings. This moment can really be the turning point of your life. It doesn't matter who you are or what obstacles you have faced—each one of us can lead a life that feels fulfilled, meaningful, and creative.

I followed my passion and took a risk that led to more opportunities and growth. I followed the light at the end of the long tunnel and made it to the other side—to become a much happier, joyful, and empowering person. You can do the same. Affirm for yourself that you can change and that you have the right and the power to do so. Read aloud the next paragraph. Read it over and over as many times as you need to until you believe it:

My passions and determination will help me succeed along my life path as long as I accept that I am not the kind of person who'll settle down to an ordinary, everyday situation. I am here to stimulate change and to broaden my own and the rest of humanity's horizons! I love to learn new things and to apply that learning to various situations in life. And I am successful at it when I do so.

Success is not about waiting for the world to tell you that you're great; it's about living your dreams and passions, no matter what they may be. You have the ultimate power to shape your destiny, so harness your power and put it into action. You no longer need to feel lost, uncertain, and held back.

When I look back at my life, I feel my greatest accomplishment is that I have found myself and gone where I needed to go. I think I'm exactly where I should be.

DARING TO CHANGE

Which life will you choose?

When you contrast the bad news, the paycheck-to-paycheck struggle that kills freedom, with the good news, the phenomenal wealth and opportunity that is all around us, you begin to realize that life is not fair. Or is it? The fact is, in life you don't get what you wish for. In life, you get what you go for. When you know your passion and gifts, you know what you're here for. Your passion and gifts are powerful and they are waiting to be released or more fully expressed. Imagine knowing your true purpose, and the difference you are here to make. What difference would that make in *your* life?

I believe it's a basic need of every human to know his or her purpose. And somewhere around mid-life, what was a nudge becomes a much bigger wake-up call if you don't take notice.

Change is the only path to your dreams because to change, you must move from here to there. We need guts to make the necessary changes in our lives to go from here to there. You have the power to create anything you want in life. You need to develop a winning formula to improve your life now and forever. Once your mind is inspired, your spirit is enlightened. Count your blessings and move forward to living your true life purpose.

You're Never Too Old to Embrace Change: Grandma Moses

How many people think, "I am too old and it's too late to start living my passion?" If you are full of passion and the courage to follow your dream, you can create the life you want at any time and any age.

Grandma Moses is the perfect example of someone who never thought she was too old to change. Born in 1860, Anna Mary Moses left home at thirteen, married, gave birth to ten children, and worked hard to raise the five who survived. After her husband died, she was struggling to make a living. Then one day, her daughter showed her a picture embroidered in yarn and challenged her to do something similar. So Anna Mary began embroidering pictures made with yarn tightly woven on fabric. In these pictures, she created beautiful folk art scenes. At age seventy-eight, her fingers became too stiff to hold a needle. But she had an artistic passion, so rather than stop creating, she decided to paint in her barn. She created brilliantly colored, beautifully detailed scenes of country life on Masonite (wood fiber board) panels. For a while, she gave these away or sold them for small amounts of money.

Then when she was seventy-nine, the art world discovered her and "Grandma Moses" became a famous folk artist. She went on to produce more than two thousand paintings. Her paintings were soon reproduced on Christmas cards, tiles, and fabrics throughout the United States and overseas. In 1949, when she was eighty-nine years old, President Harry S. Truman presented her with the Women's National Press Club trophy for outstanding accomplishment in art. In 1952, at age ninety-two, she published her autobiography and titled it *Grandma Moses: My Life's History*. And in her one-hundredth year, she completed her book illustrations for the classic poem *'Twas the Night before Christmas*. Today, some of her paintings sell at auction for over one million dollars.

If Grandma Moses could begin a new career and succeed when she was nearly eighty, doing something she absolutely loved to do, then you can work on your dream and succeed at any time and any age as well.

What would your life be if you had no courage to attempt any change? We have one life to live! Plant the seed, take action, and visualize that it's coming now! This is your time. Your destiny awaits. Ready yourself and begin. Make your life a fascinating adventure for yourself and others.

Dare Questions

Are you doing what you love to do in life?

_____

_____

Who are you seeking approval from today?

_____

_____

If you didn't seek others' approval, what would you do with your life?

_____

_____

_____

_____

Are you following your passion to live the life you want?

_____

_____

_____

Is your work aligned with your vision?

_____

_____

_____

DARING TO CHANGE

Are you inspired by what you do? If not, what is stopping you from making a change?

_____
_____
_____
_____

What do you want to be remembered for in life?

_____
_____
_____

Are you inspired now to change and follow your dream?

_____
_____
_____

A FINAL NOTE

Will You Change?

You've now reached the end of this book. I congratulate you for beginning to read this book and thinking that change might be possible for you. I especially congratulate you for finishing the book and thinking about the Dare Questions at the end of each chapter.

I have one question left for you. Now that you have read this book, will that be the end of it, or are you going to dare to change?

Are you ready now to change? You should be. I've told you everything you need to know to make your change successful. Think of these steps as a roadmap to your destination. Begin where you are now by determining your deepest desires and charting the course you need. How will you make the changes necessary to arrive where you want to be in life?

DARING TO CHANGE

Here is a summary of the directions you need to take to make your change happen.

THE DARING TO CHANGE ROADMAP

1. Discover your deepest desires.
2. Believe in yourself.
3. Take a risk in spite of your fears.
4. Find your spirit of adventure.
5. Create your vision and set your intentions.
6. Turn obstacles and adversities into your strengths.
7. Enjoy synchronicities as a sign that God is co-creating with you.
8. Know that you have the power to move mountains to make your dreams come true.
9. Be persistent. Never give up.
10. Make your passion into your life purpose.
11. Be courageous.
12. Do what you love to live the life you want.

Following this roadmap will help you arrive at the destination of the life you want.

If you are still feeling overwhelmed, then I ask you whether maybe you have decided that you really don't want to change.

A Final Note

Maybe you prefer staying in your comfort zone. After all, if you are perfectly happy, there is no reason to change. If you think you don't need to change, then ask yourself the following questions. If you can say "Yes" to any of them, then I guess you don't need or want to change after all.

1. Am I perfectly happy, and do I believe that no greater happiness is possible for me?
2. Am I completely content in my relationships with other people and I don't want more or improved relationships?
3. Am I satisfied with my job—do I get up every morning looking forward to the work I do?
4. Am I completely satisfied with my income? Do I never worry about money or feel like there is nothing I could possibly want to buy or enjoy if I had more money?
5. Do I have all the time I want to achieve and do what I want in life?
6. Do I feel completely safe and protected so that no unexpected event could ever upset or even startle me?
7. Will people continue to find me interesting and fun to be with if I never change or try anything new?
8. Am I going to be happy for the rest of my life without making any changes?
9. Will I have no regrets in my life if I die tomorrow?
10. Will I leave my family, friends, and the world a better place if I do not make any changes?

DARING TO CHANGE

I bet you didn't answer "Yes" to a single one of those questions. And I bet you knew I wasn't really serious about asking them. My point is that you know if you don't make the change you are thinking and dreaming about making, you will regret it. And you don't want to wait too long to make a change and then discover it is too late. The time to change is now. Begin today even if it's just in a small way. Small steps will add up until your change leads to the big goals and achievements that you are dreaming can happen.

Perhaps you want to change but you still need a little help. Perhaps you need to go back and read this book again. Perhaps you need to read several other books and attend seminars like I did before you feel inspired. Then you will feel the spark within you—the spark that will tell you what your passion is and inspire you to take that scary step, the step that takes courage but is necessary when you want to change.

I know you can do it. God knows you can do it. Remember, He is your co-creator. Remember that if I could do it, you can too.

The answer for how to change is already within you. I encourage you to look for it, to pray for the answer to come to you, and to trust that it will come. You know you need to change, and you need to make the effort to change. Do you want to be in the same place next year as you are now? Or do

A Final Note

you want something different in your life? It's time to make that change, or at least to plan to make it.

Before you close this book, make a plan. Create your own personalized roadmap for change with your own directions and destinations along the way. I challenge you here and now to write down the five things you are going to do, big and small, to make a change. And I challenge you to give yourself a reasonable deadline to accomplish each one. Go ahead and write them down now:

To Change My Life To Pursue My Dream, I Will:

1. _____ by (insert date) _____.

2. _____ by (insert date) _____.

3. _____ by (insert date) _____.

4. _____ by (insert date) _____.

5. _____ by (insert date) _____.

Now that you have a plan, your own personalized change roadmap, are you ready to take the leap? Go ahead. What are you waiting for? You know if you don't, you'll end up regretting it. Take the leap. I promise the landing will be much smoother than you fear.

In the long run, perseverance with clear vision will always pay off, no matter what obstacles you face or how lofty your vision may be. Under any circumstances, the power of clear vision, perseverance, and meaningful coincidence will make even your seemingly impossible dreams a reality.

In closing, I wish you much success and many blessings in daring to change to create the life you want. Dream boldly—you have everything you need within you to fulfill your highest visions.

If you want additional help, please contact me through my website **www.DaringtoChange.com** for a complimentary thirty-minute consultation to help you begin to make the changes you want and need to in your life.

Go ahead! Dare to change! And enjoy every minute of it!

About the Author

HELEN YOON is an author, speaker, empowerment workshop leader, and coach. After daring to change and succeeding many times in her life, Helen Yoon now helps others make the changes they need to live the life they want.

For over twenty-five years, Helen Yoon served as an award-winning Elementary School Teacher, Mentor, Administrator for the Los Angeles Unified School District, and Adjunct Professor for the Korean Bilingual Teacher Training Program at California State University, Los Angeles. In 1984, Helen was the recipient of the Overseas Educator of the Year Award from the President of Korea.

Helen Yoon grew up during the Korean War, almost permanently losing her mother in the chaos. After college, she pursued her dream of being an "independent and respected woman" with further education in the U.S.

Daring to change, Helen went to Los Angeles, California, where she knew no one, to attend graduate school. She supported herself while she earned a Master's Degree in Education with a teaching credential. She recalls God co-created with her every step of the way.

Helen's life is a testament of how to change for the better and how your dream or larger purpose is always possible. She lives in Santa Monica, California.

You can visit Helen Yoon at www.DaringToChange.com

www.ingramcontent.com/pod-product-compliance
Lightning Source LLC
Chambersburg PA
CBHW061300110426
42742CB00012BA/1995